DESERTED DREAMS

CALIFORNIA'S ABANDONED OASIS

KEVIN LACY

—
AMERICA
—
THROUGH
—
TIME

Published by America Through Time®
An imprint of Sutton Publishing Inc
www.through-time.com

First published 2025
Copyright © Kevin Lacy 2025

ISBN 978-1-62545-161-3

Typeset in Trade Gothic 10pt on 15pt
Printed and bound in the United States of America

ACKNOWLEDGMENTS

Creating this book would not have been possible without the support and encouragement of my family and friends. Foremost, I would like to thank my wife, Kelly, for supporting my desire to stop at every abandoned place I see and being extremely patient as I run around trying to find the best composition for the perfect photo. Your countless hours of waiting for me have not gone unnoticed. To my parents, thank you for encouraging me to follow my own path and for sticking by my side in every crazy and unconventional turn my life has taken. You have always been extremely supportive of whatever I do. I would also like to acknowledge an influential group of artists in my life, who have shown me that you can create a life around the art that you love and that has shaped me into the person I have become today, Catherine Lacy, Barbara Fox, Shari Lacy, and Deb McGowan. Your influence means more to me than you know, and I thank you.

AUTHOR'S NOTE

Urban exploring, or the experience of exploring abandoned places, is becoming an increasingly popular activity. It draws in enthusiasts with the allure of abandoned buildings, forgotten structures, and the remnants of bygone eras. The fascination lies in the opportunity to uncover hidden histories, witness the passage of time through decaying architecture, and experience the unique atmosphere of neglected spaces.

The attraction to urban exploring often stems from a sense of curiosity and a desire to discover the untold stories that once lied behind closed doors. Explorers are drawn to the mystery of forgotten places, each with its own narrative waiting to be uncovered. These places, once full of life, are now canvases where time has painted a vivid portrait of neglect, offering a seldom-seen glimpse into the past.

However, the thrill of urban exploring comes with inherent dangers, and enthusiasts must tread cautiously to ensure both their own safety and the preservation of the sites they explore. Abandoned structures may pose structural hazards, such as weakened floors or unstable walls. In addition, there's the risk of encountering environmental hazards such as mold, asbestos, or dangerous other pollutants. As such, safety should be a top priority for urban explorers.

To navigate these dangers while still enjoying the activity, aspiring urban explorers should adhere to several key safety measures. First and foremost, it is essential to conduct thorough research about the chosen location including its history, structural integrity, and potential other risks. Equipping oneself with proper safety gear such as sturdy footwear, gloves, and a mask is crucial for protection.

Never explore alone, as having a reliable partner can be a lifeline in case of an emergency. Informing someone about the planned exploration, including the location and estimated return time adds an extra layer of precaution. Urban explorers should also exercise respect for the places they visit, refraining from vandalism or theft to preserve the historical integrity of the site.

While urban exploring offers a unique perspective on the past, safety should always be the priority. By approaching the activity with caution, preparation, and a deep respect for the places visited, enthusiasts can enjoy the thrill of uncovering forgotten histories while minimizing the associated risks.

The author and the publisher of this book are in no way promoting trespassing on private property, or any other illegal activity that may arise during the act of urban exploration. Always adhere to local laws, and if you do decide to venture into abandoned spaces, please exercise caution.

CONTENTS

INTRODUCTION

The California desert stands as a testament to the ever-changing balance between human ambition and the unforgiving forces of nature. From the early settlers who ventured into this arid wilderness seeking their fortunes in gold, to the economic boom that saw towns spring up like mirages in the sand, the California desert has been both a canvas of dreams and a stage for harsh realities. It was a land that promised fortune, a fresh start, and endless possibilities. As pioneers moved westward, they soon discovered that beneath the sunbaked earth lay treasures beyond just gold, treasures that led to prosperity and thriving communities.

Today, the California desert has hundreds of small towns dotting the arid landscape. However, the very essence of desert life that attracts people to this challenging terrain is often the force that ultimately caused them to abandon their dreams.

With its vast and seemingly desolate expanses, the desert is home to numerous abandoned places that bear witness to the ebb and flow of human activity. Understanding the reasons behind the abandonment of these sites unveils a complex tapestry woven with economic, environmental, and societal threads.

There are several reasons that places featured in this book have become forgotten. Economic factors often play a pivotal role in the abandonment of locations in the California desert. Industries that once thrived in these arid landscapes, such as mining and agriculture, sometimes faced fluctuations in profitability. As resource extraction became less lucrative, communities built around these industries struggled to sustain themselves.

Environmental challenges further contribute to the abandonment of certain areas in the California desert. Harsh climatic conditions, including extreme temperatures and limited water resources, can make it difficult for settlements to flourish. In some instances, environmental degradation, such as soil erosion or the encroachment of sand dunes, may render a location uninhabitable, prompting the departure of residents.

The evolution of transportation networks is another factor influencing the abandonment of desert locales. As infrastructure and roads shifted over time, some settlements found themselves isolated or bypassed, leading to a decline in economic opportunities and population. Remote desert towns, once vibrant stops along travel routes, may become obsolete as highways are rerouted, diverting traffic away from their doorsteps.

Additionally, societal changes, such as shifts in lifestyle preferences or demographic patterns, contribute to the abandonment of certain desert areas. As urbanization and technological advancements lure populations toward more modernized centers, smaller communities in the desert may struggle to retain residents and vital services, eventually resulting in abandonment.

Exploring the remnants of human habitation in the California desert serves as a tangible reminder of the delicate balance between nature and civilization. The deserted structures and forgotten communities tell stories of resilience, adaptation, and the unsustainability of human endeavors in the face of the unforgiving desert environment.

Deserted Dreams takes a journey through the remnants of this exodus, uncovering the abandoned places of the California desert. Each ghost town, deserted mining camp, and crumbling structure speaks of deferred dreams and the complex relationship between humanity and the unyielding beauty of the California desert.

In the following pages we will explore the remnants of Lake Delores, a family retreat, which evolved into America's first waterpark. Take a journey down an unforgiving stretch of rail-line nicknamed "the impossible railroad." Explore abandoned roadside motels that have been forgotten by time. Discover a desert outpost with a dark and sinister history and take a photographic journey into an abandoned steel mine with over 400 dilapidated structures.

Join us as we explore the abandoned, the forgotten, and the enigmatic in this captivating saga of the rise, fall, and enduring allure of the California desert.

1

THE BACK ROADS: TAKING THE ROAD LESS TRAVELED

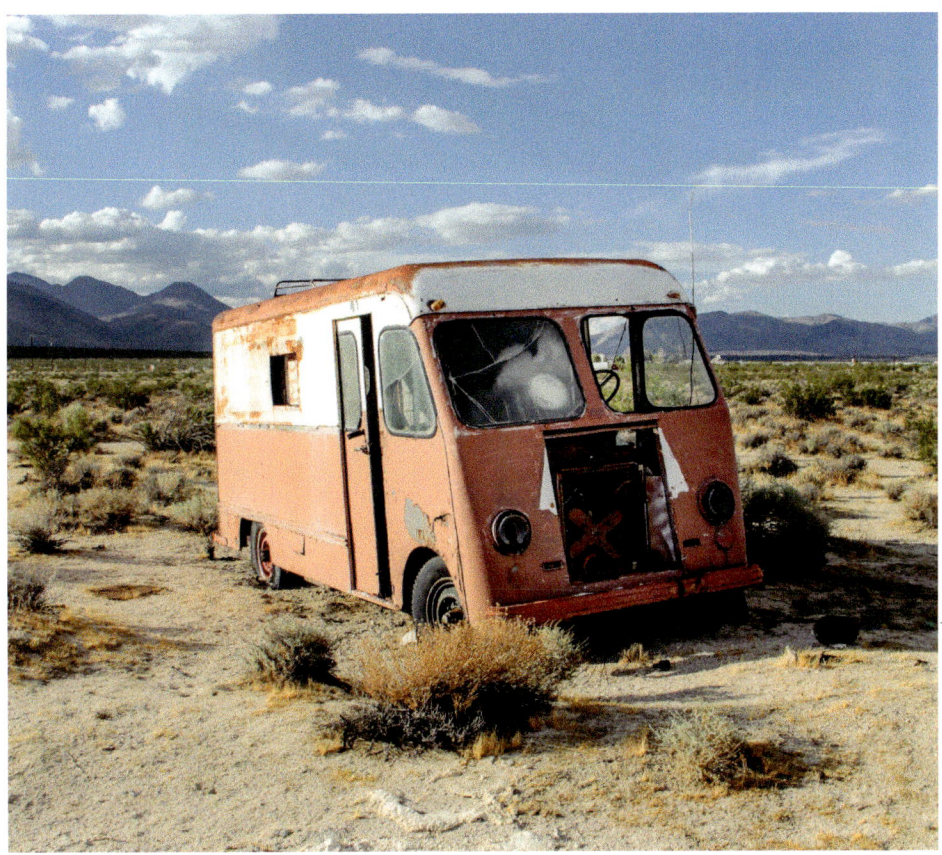

This delivery truck was next to an abandoned home. Most likely left behind when the owners moved.

A quarter of the land in California, roughly 40,000 square miles, is designated as desert terrain, an expanse that stands out as the least inhabited in the state. Here, hidden amid forgotten backroads the roads seem to extend endlessly into the arid landscape.

Initially appearing desolate, this vast territory harbors many hidden gems. This chapter dives into these forgotten roads, shedding light on what unfolds when veering off the familiar paths. These less-traveled roads navigate through a challenging landscape. The scarcity of water adds an element of survival to the journey, turning it into an exercise in endurance.

As one ventures down the road less traveled, a sense of isolation sets in, accentuated by the absence of human habitation. Amid this solitude lie relics of the past, abandoned structures, forgotten vehicles, businesses that have long ago shut their doors for the last time.

This chapter exposes the allure of less-traveled routes, uncovering the hidden treasures within the state's least inhabited region.

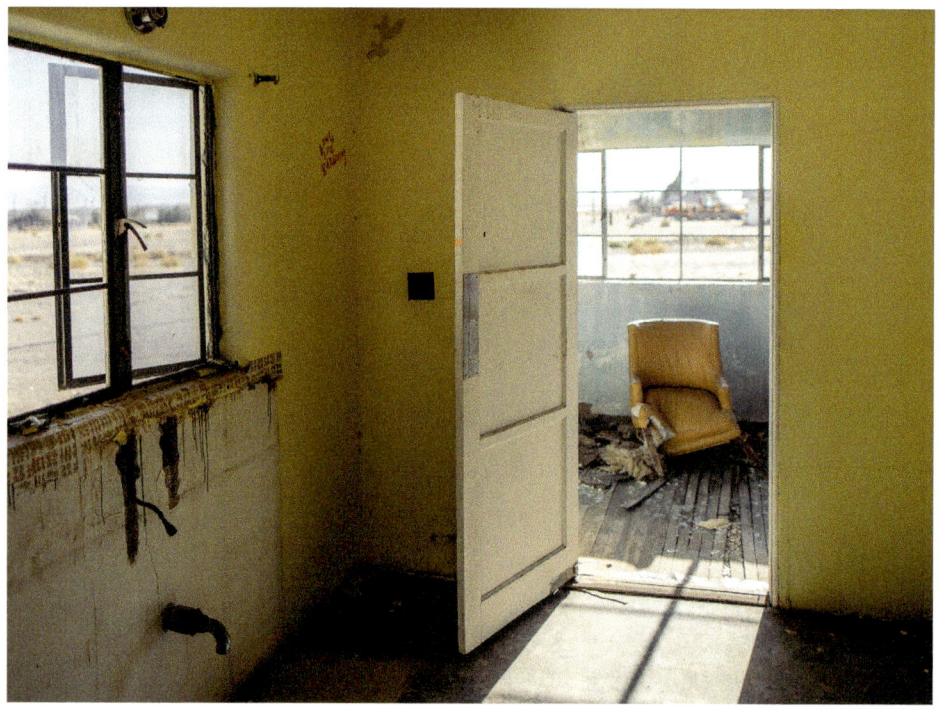

While walking the halls of an abandoned home, this chair framed up perfectly with the sunshine coming through the window.

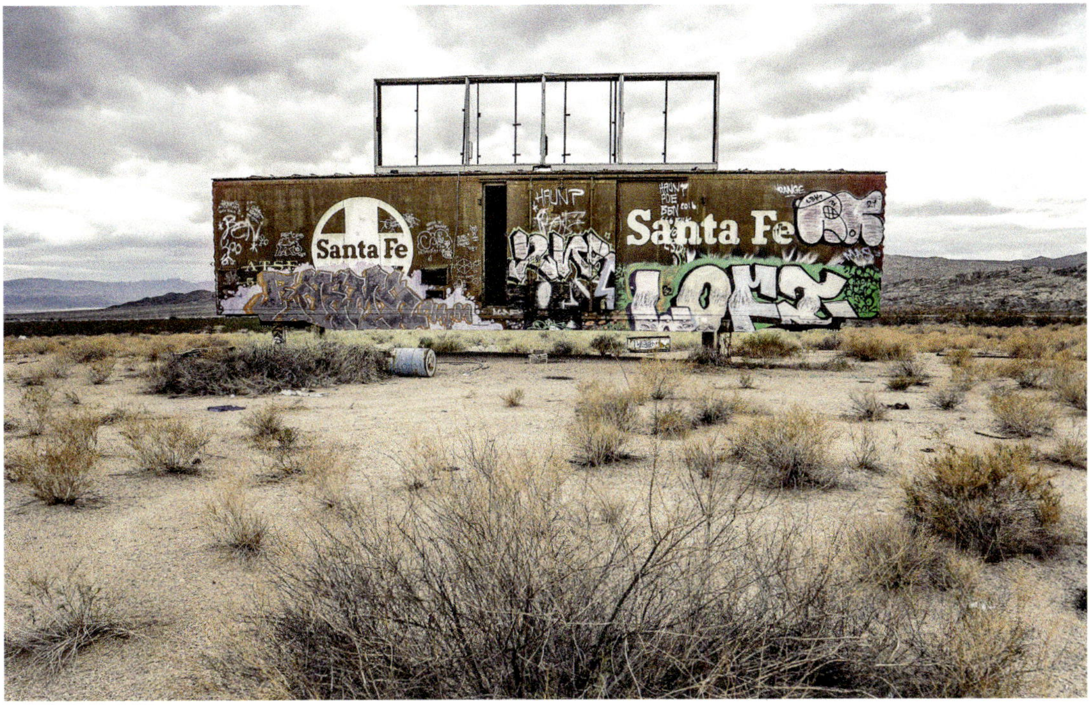

Placing semi-truck trailers or old railcars is a popular and inexpensive form of advertising along major highways. This one has been long forgotten.

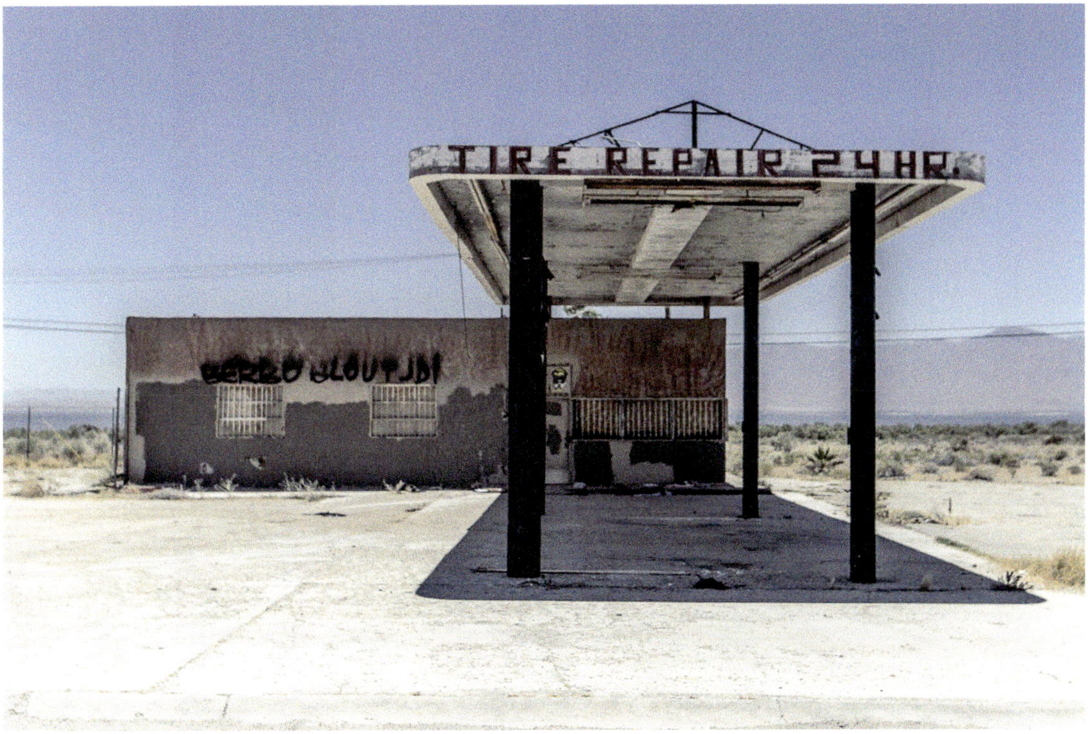

A service station at a once popular tourist destination.

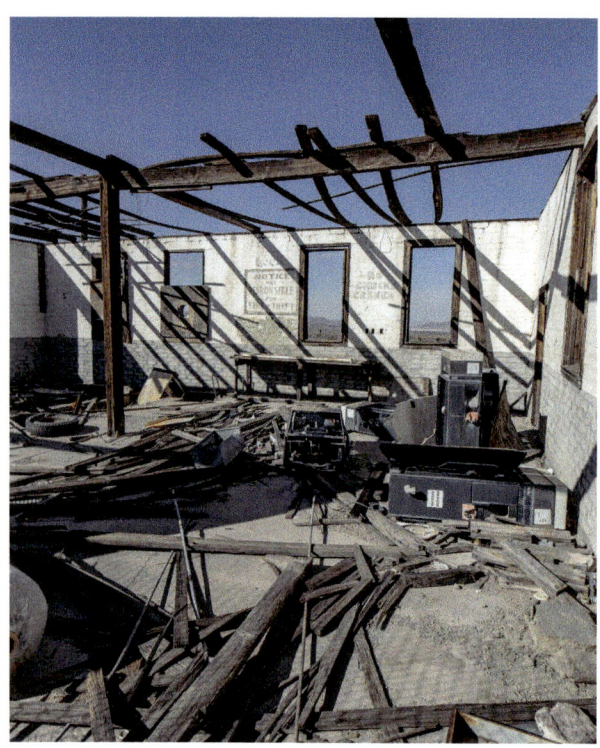

Left: The remnants of an automobile repair shop along Route 66.

Below: This motel was demolished a long time ago, but the sign remains.

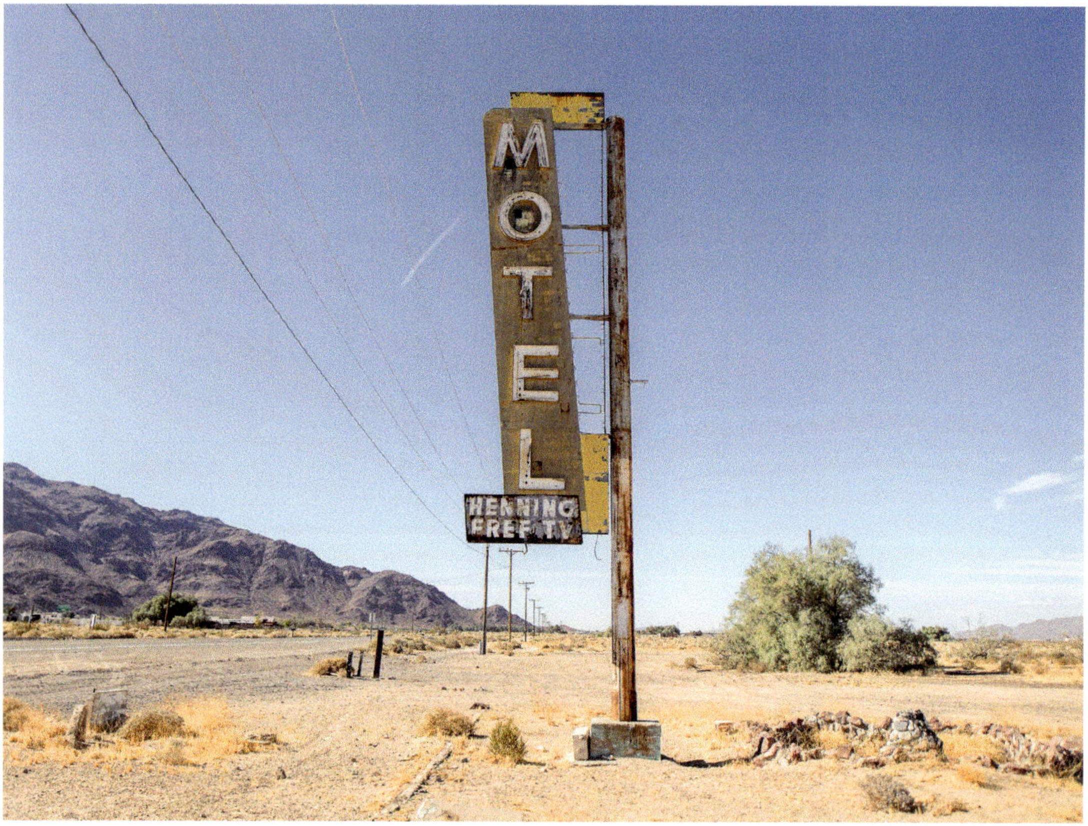

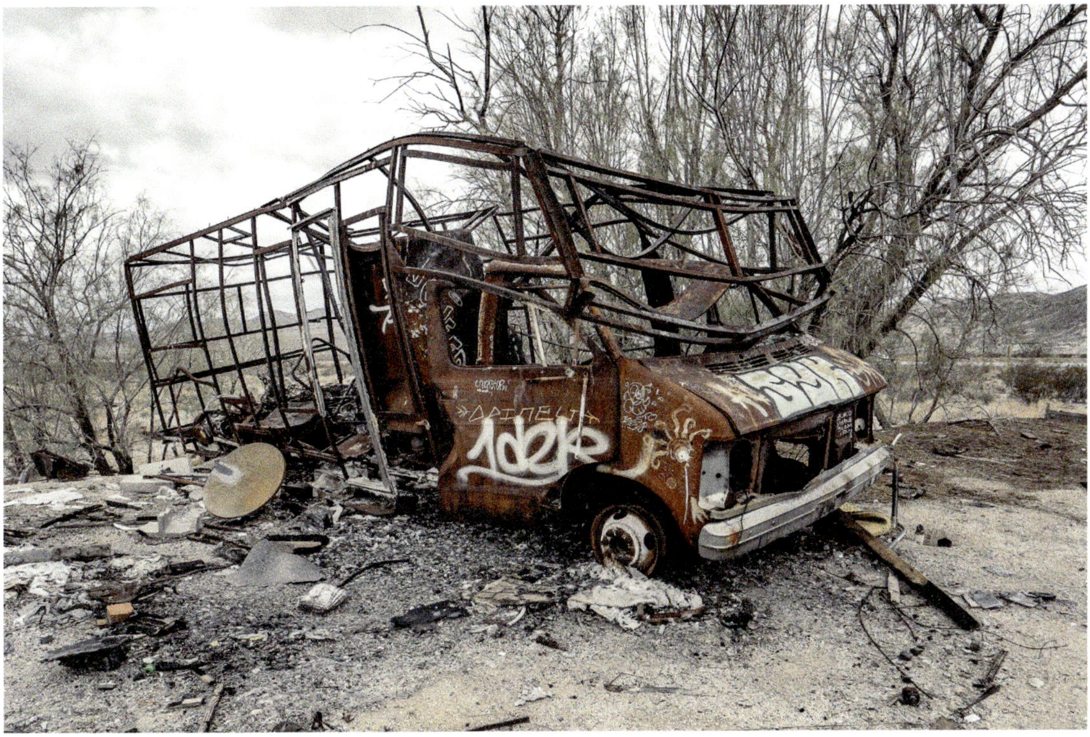

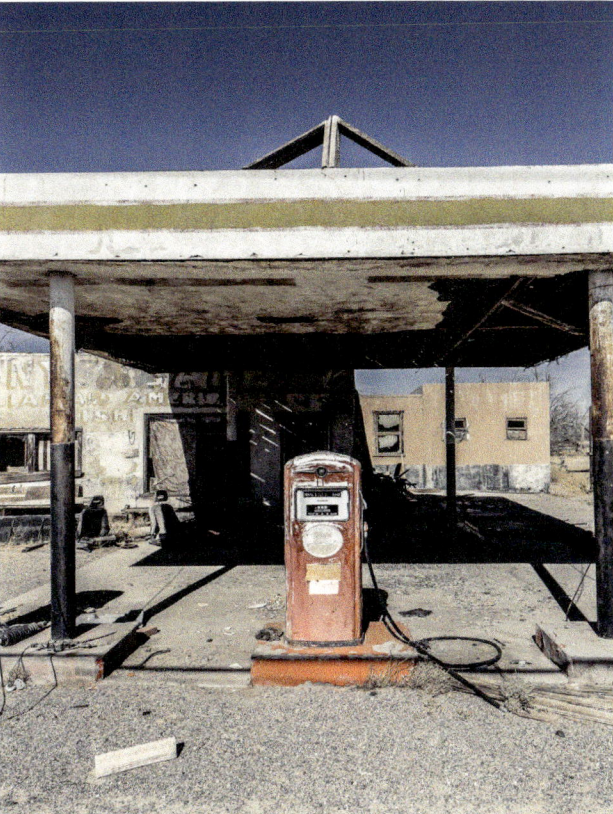

Above: This RV was probably someone's home at one time, but a fire destroyed the vehicle. The flames must have been very hot, as it warped the over cab section of the camper.

Right: Another forgotten gas station with a unique gas pump.

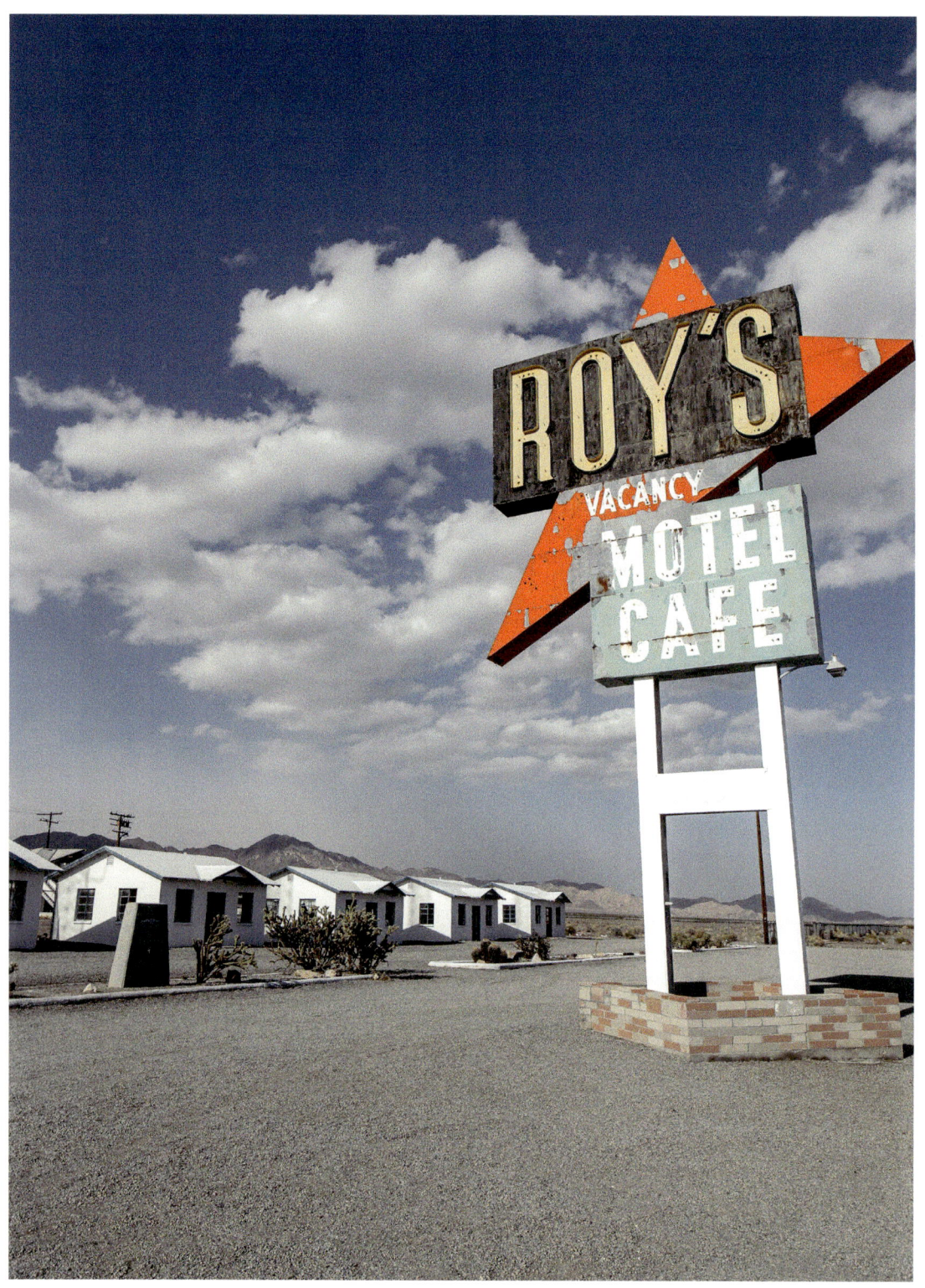

Roy's Motel and Café was once a vibrant stop for travelers on the journey to Los Angeles on Route 66. The hotel is now closed.

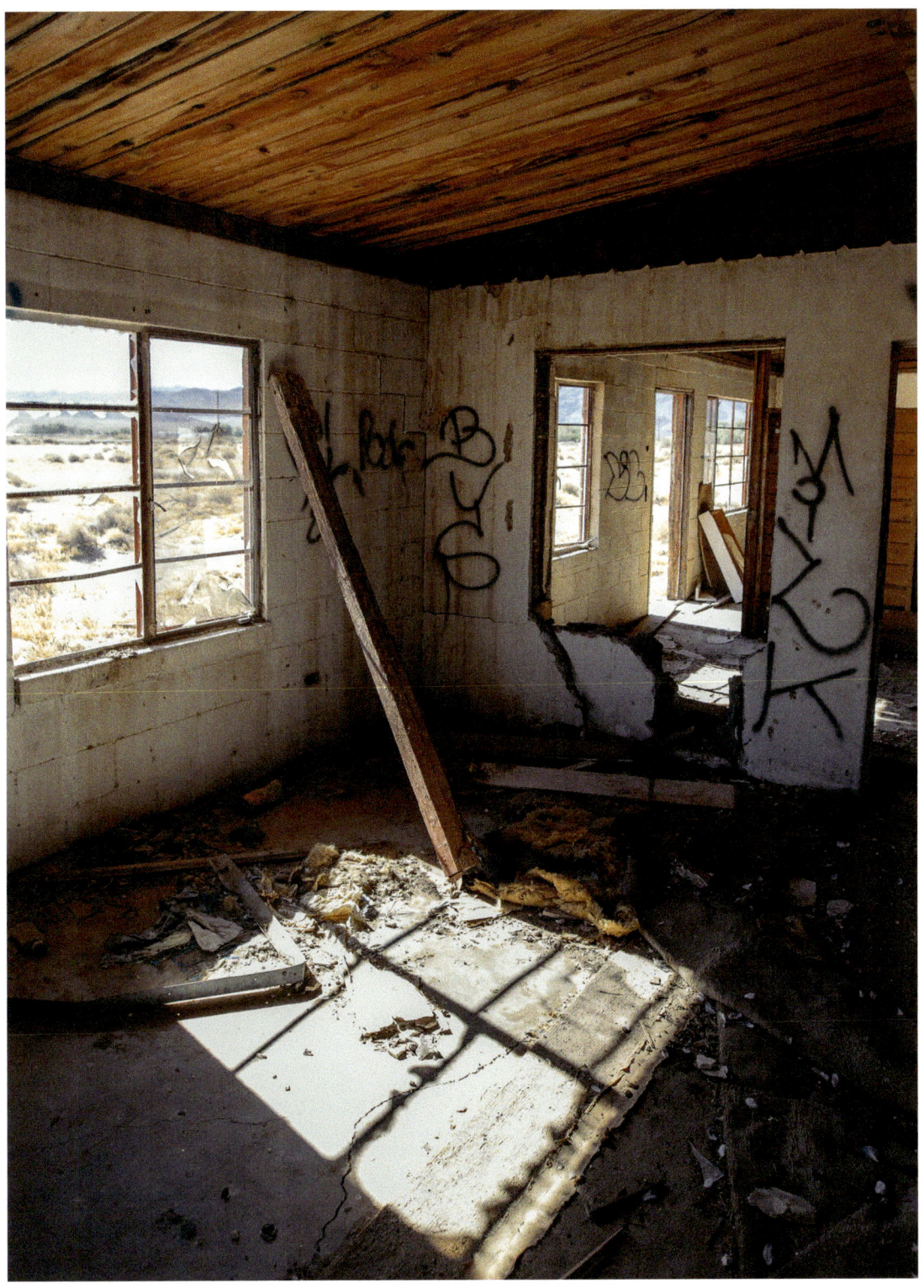

A forgotten home, being overtaken by the elements.

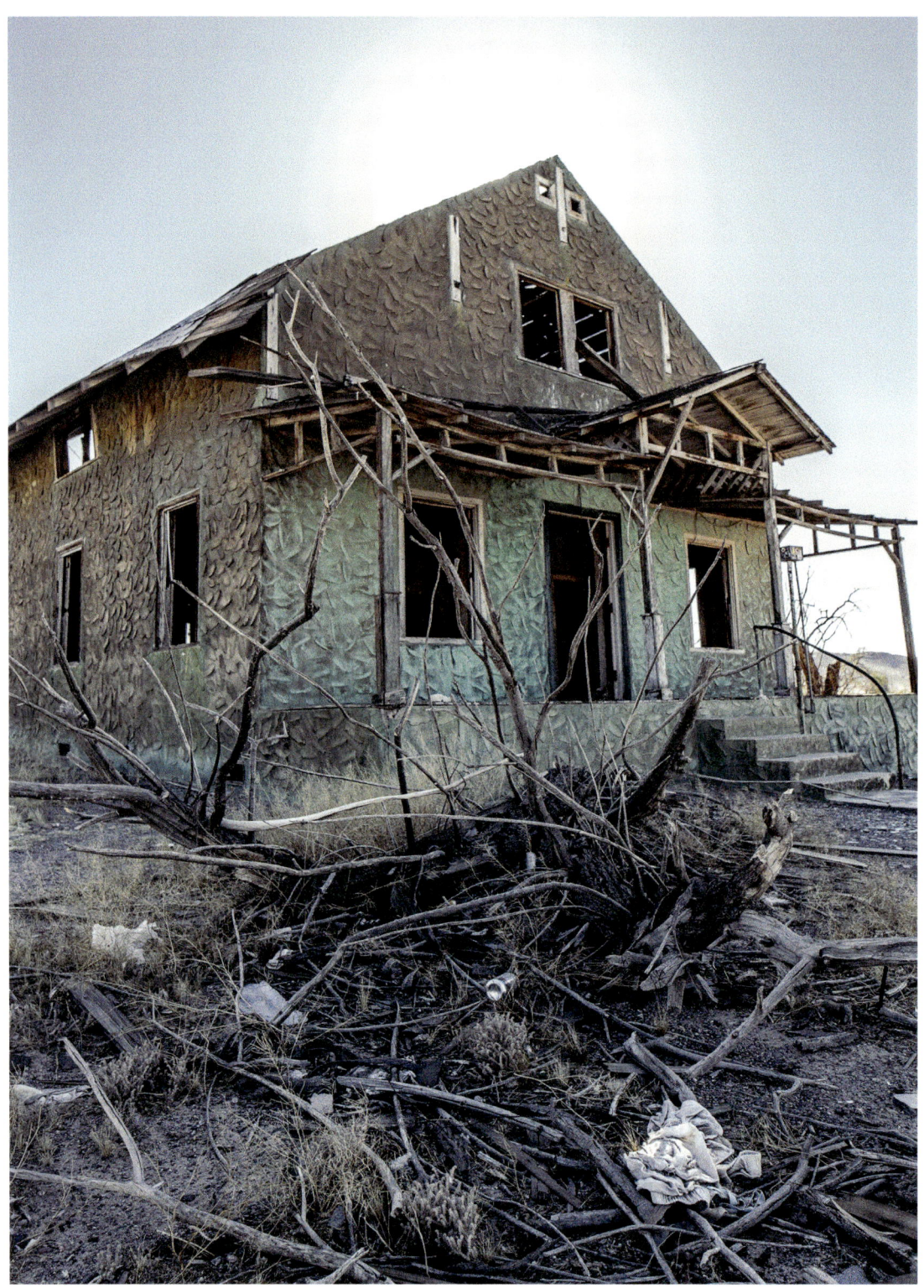

This abandoned home will probably not be standing for much longer. The roof is starting to collapse, and you can see how the harsh desert environment is really taking its toll on the building.

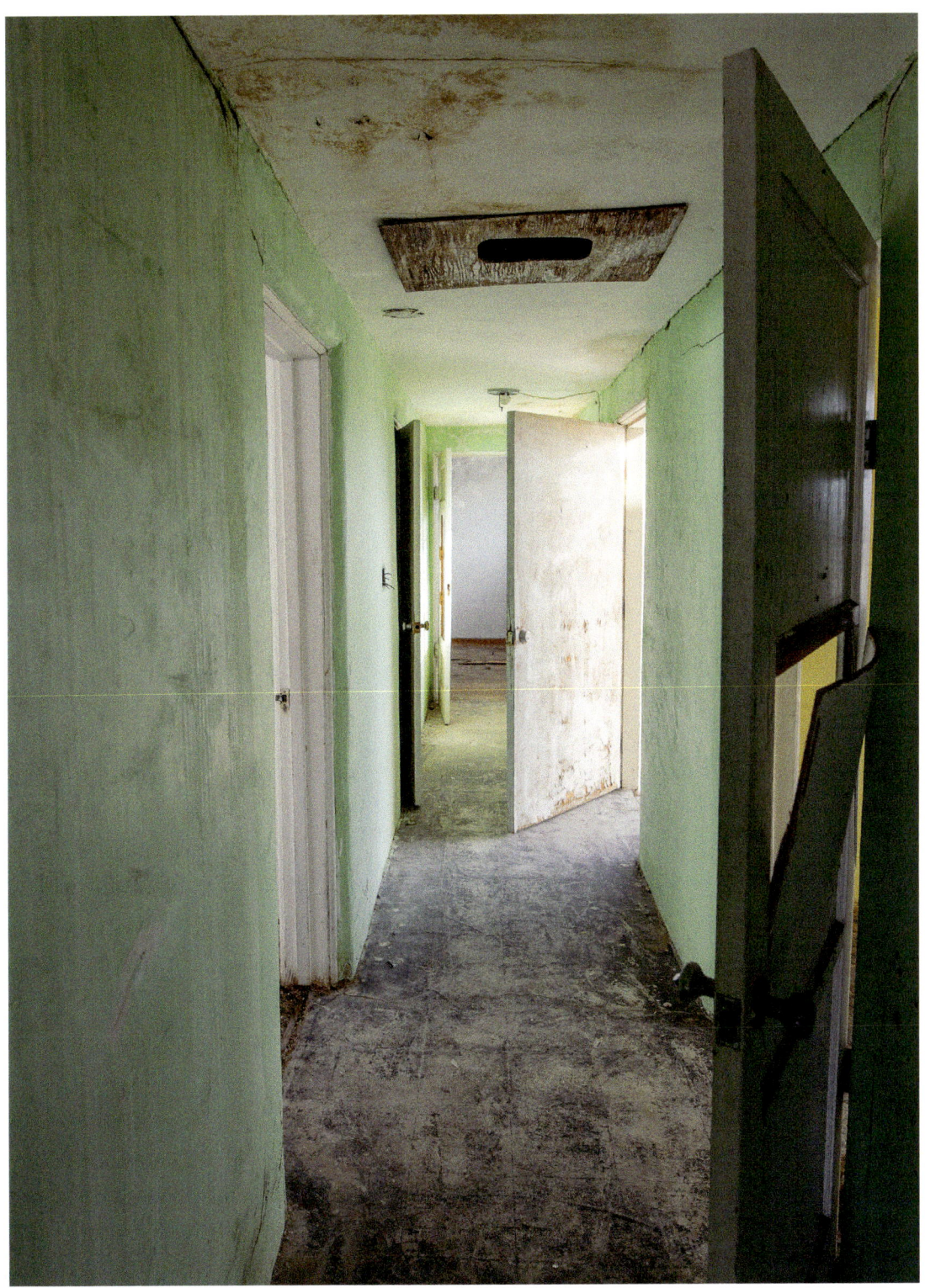

A colorful hallway of an abandoned residence.

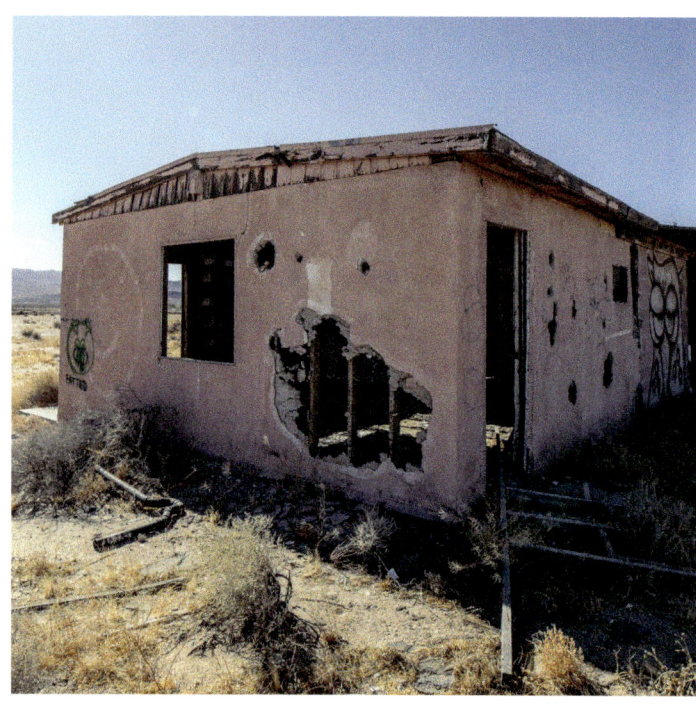

On this building, you can see the method of construction. Chicken wire was used to adhere the plaster to the walls.

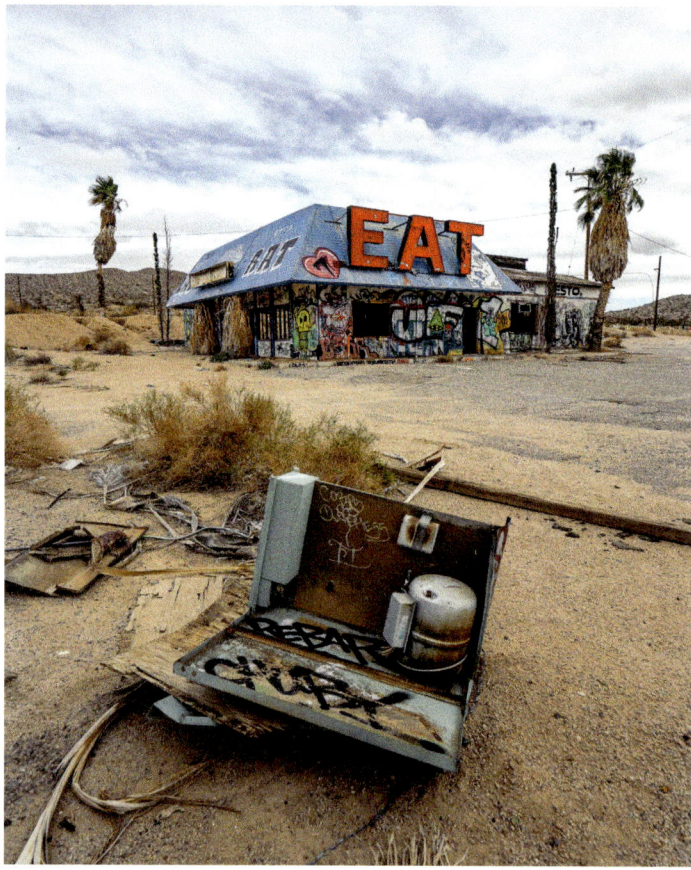

This restaurant once lured people in from the freeway with its giant letters.

2

THE IMPOSSIBLE RAILROAD: NAVIGATING THE CARRIZO GORGE

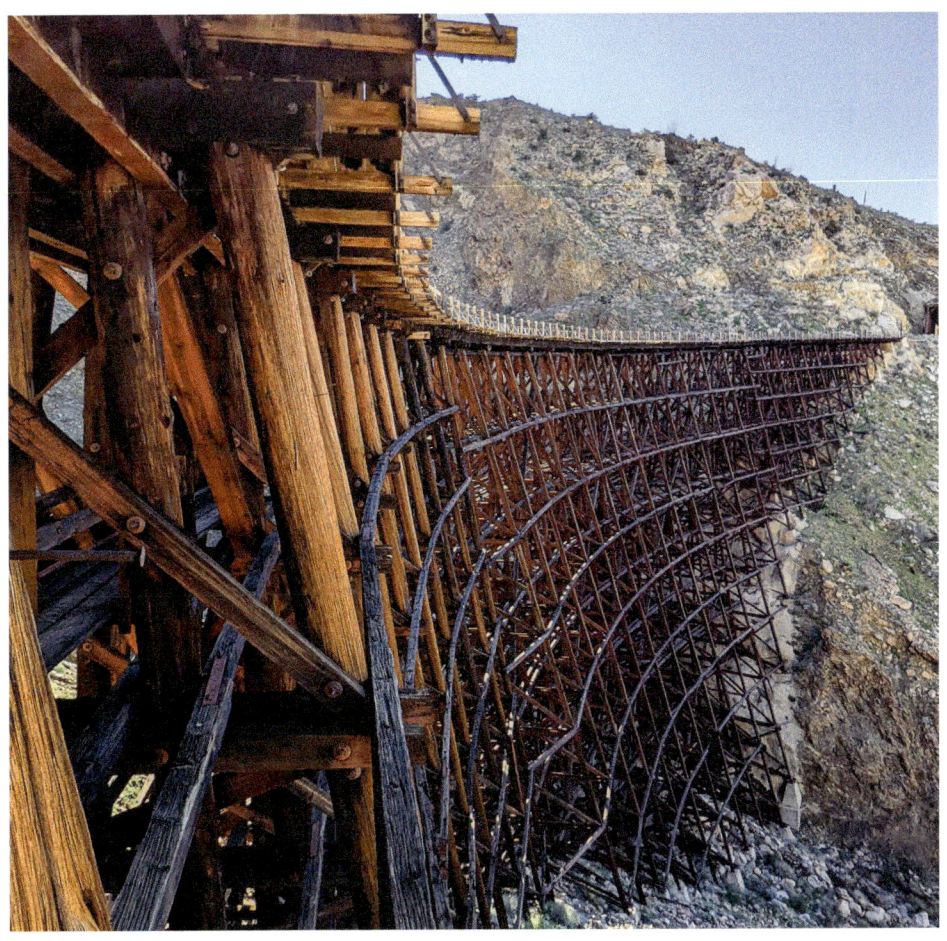

The Goat Canyon trestle bridge is the largest wooden trestle bridge ever created.

Deep in the California Desert lies a stretch of railway nicknamed "the Impossible Railroad." This railroad line would connect California to Arizona, and thus connecting this part of California to the rest of the country's eastern markets. However, one stretch of this railroad posed a problem. Traversing the challenging terrain of the Carrizo Gorge was troublesome. During the planning stages of this railroad, engineers called this section of the route "impossible" for the immense logistical challenges involved. Crossing the steep and rugged terrain of the Jacumba Mountains would require the line to pass seventeen tunnels and fourteen wooden trestle bridges to navigate locomotives safely through the 11-mile stretch. Despite concerns, construction began in 1907, and it would take twelve years until the entire line was complete.

The railroad experienced a series of difficulties, with several of the tunnels collapsing over the next few decades, including an earthquake that caused the collapse of tunnel 15 in 1932. The collapse was so big that it could not be repaired. To bypass tunnel 15, an all-wood trestle bridge was constructed from redwood timber. Wood was chosen for the material of this bridge as a metal bridge could not withstand the temperature fluctuations in this area of the desert. In the summer, temperatures can reach higher than 120 degrees Fahrenheit. Whereas in the winter, the temperatures regularly plummet below the freezing point. The trestle bridge is 633 feet long, 183 feet tall, and is the world's largest all wood trestle bridge to ever be created.

To resist the canyon's high winds, the bridge was built with a 14-degree curve. Construction of the bridge was completed by 1933, allowing the railroad route to resume operation. The risk of fire was a major concern for the owners of the railroad line due to the arid climate, so a fire suppression tank car was installed next to the bridge located close to the start of tunnel 16.

The rail line was used for the next few decades, but due to the increased popularity of automobile traffic, scheduled passenger service was suspended in the 1950s. Freight travel continued for several years, despite the line being closed periodically due to damage from the elements and more tunnel collapses. The line closed indefinitely in 2008. Since that time, two more tunnels have collapsed along the route.

Today the area is a popular destination for hikers and mountain bikers. Along the route there are multiple abandoned trains, wooden bridges and collapsed tunnels.

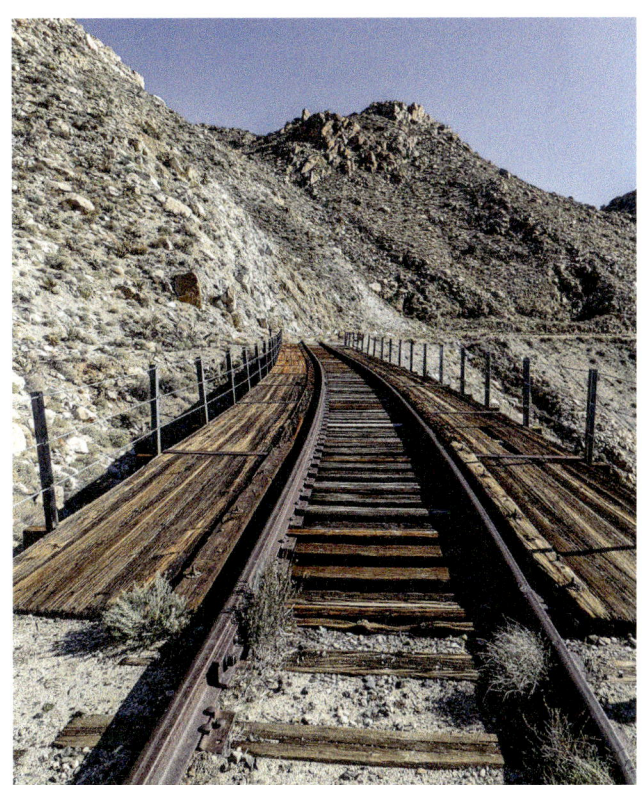

One of the many wooden bridges on the impossible railroad.

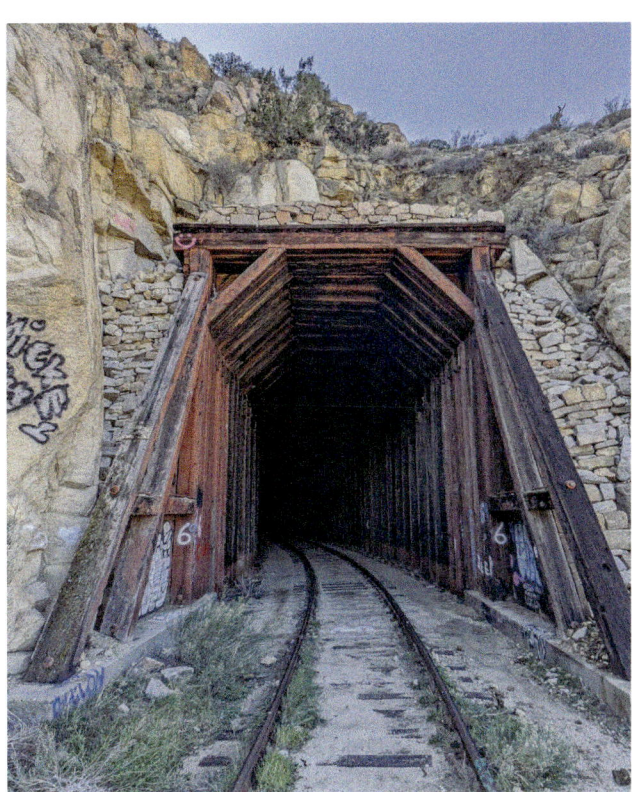

The entrance to tunnel number 6.

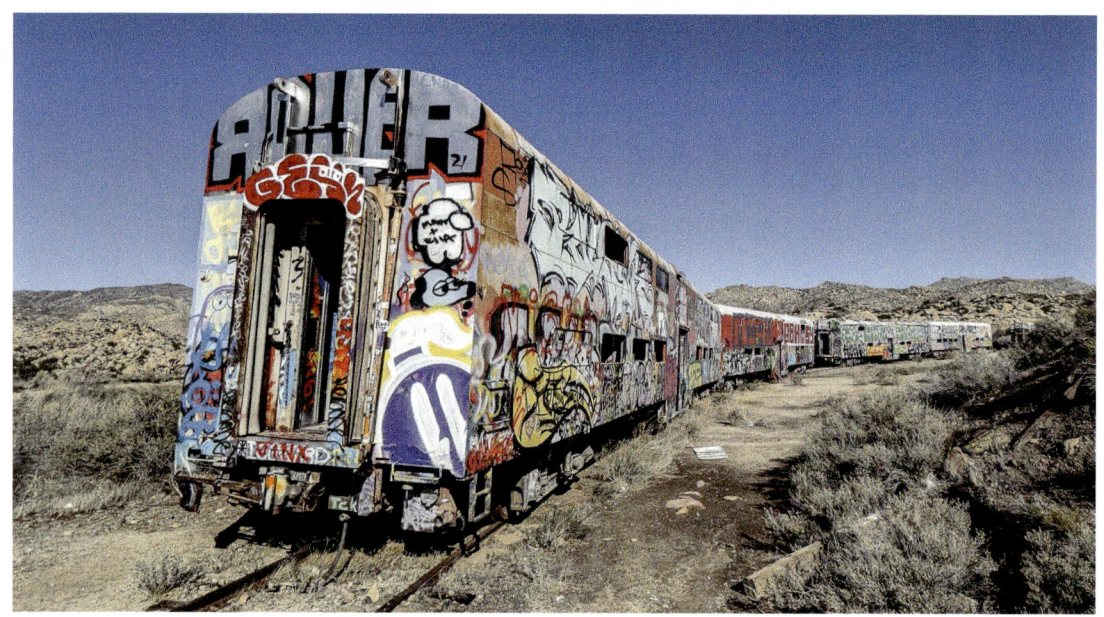

Bi-level passenger train cars, on a spur off the main line.

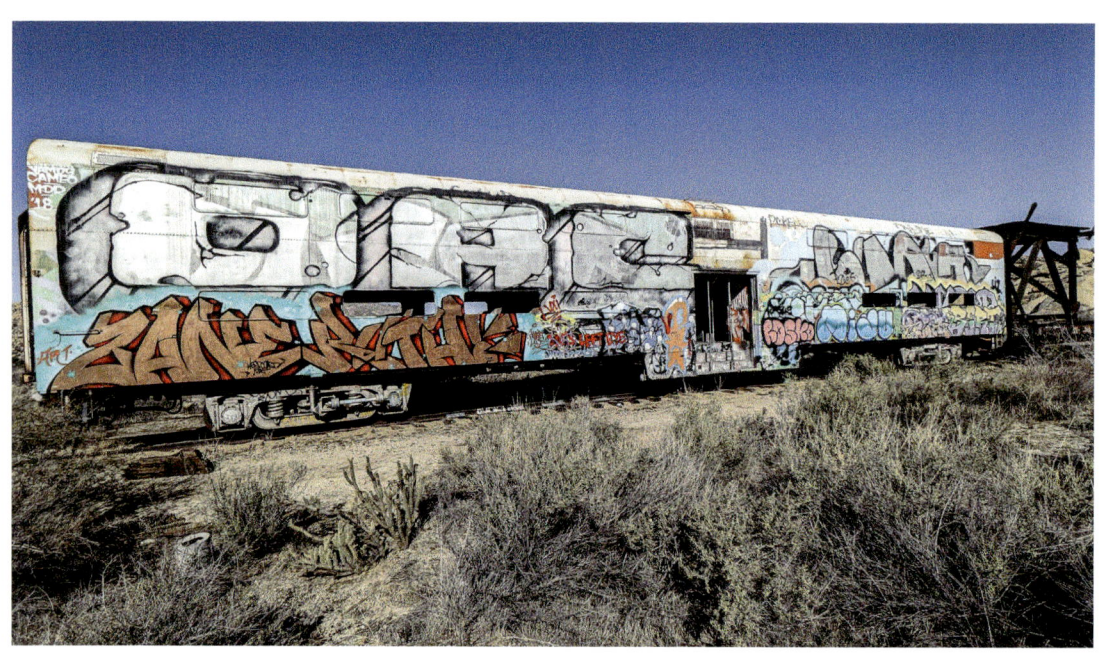

These train cars have become a canvas for graffiti artists.

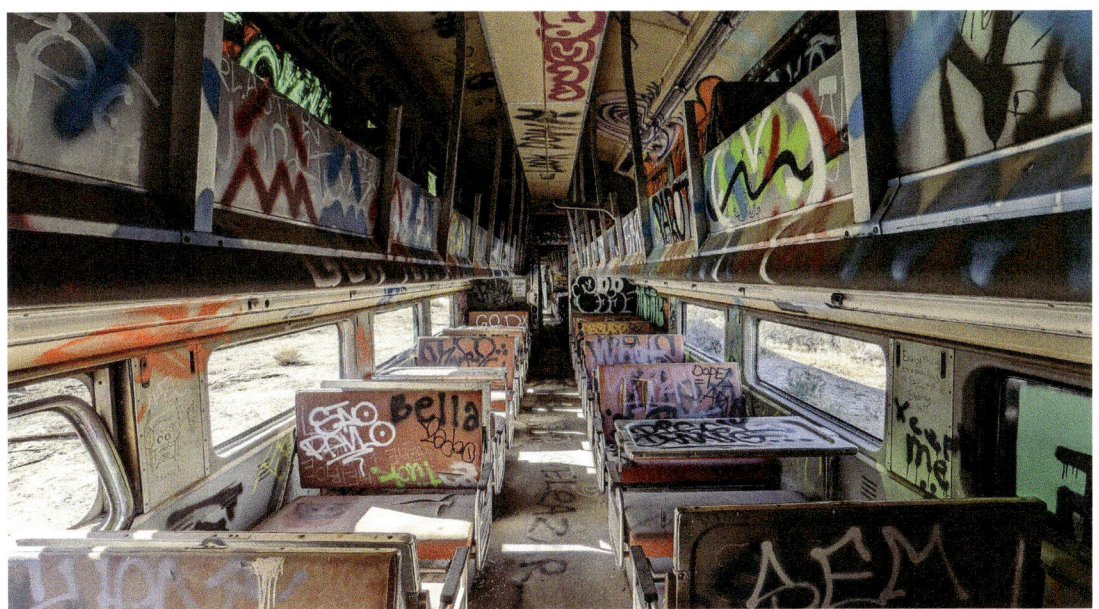

Above: Interior of one of the bi-level passenger train cars.

Right: Single passenger car, sitting on rusted train tracks.

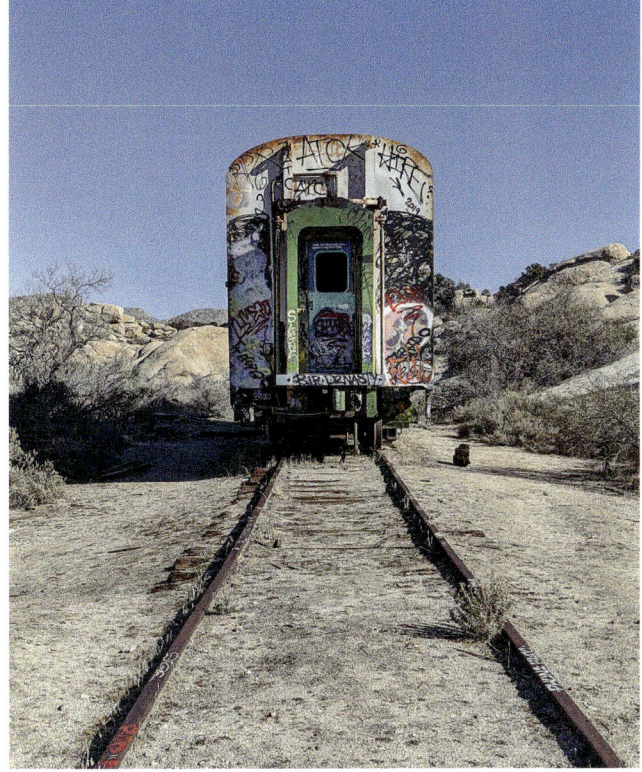

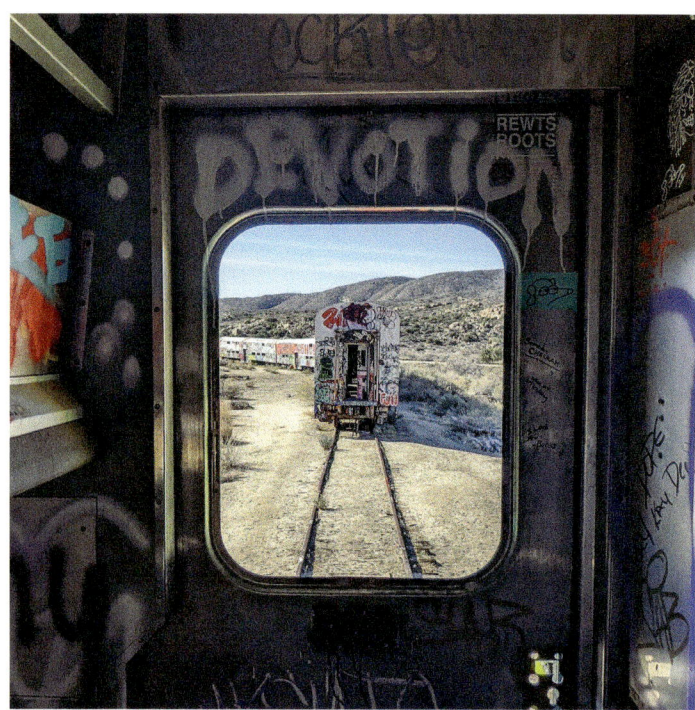

While walking through the passenger cars, I saw this perfectly framed composition of the next section of train cars.

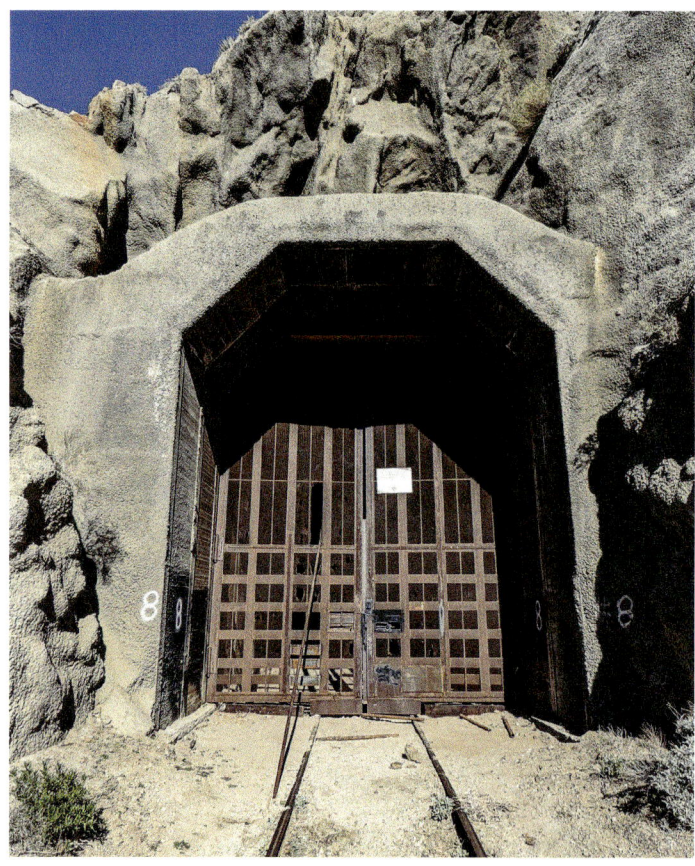

Tunnel number 8 has been closed due to a collapse.

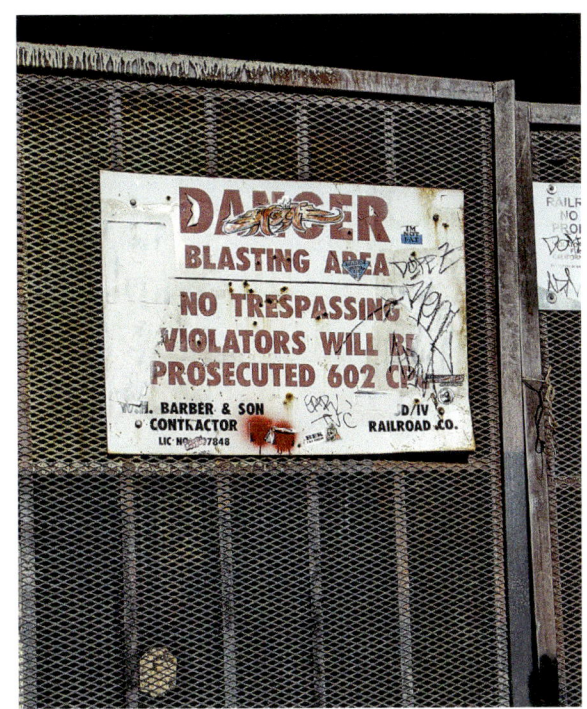

The sign on another collapsed tunnel.

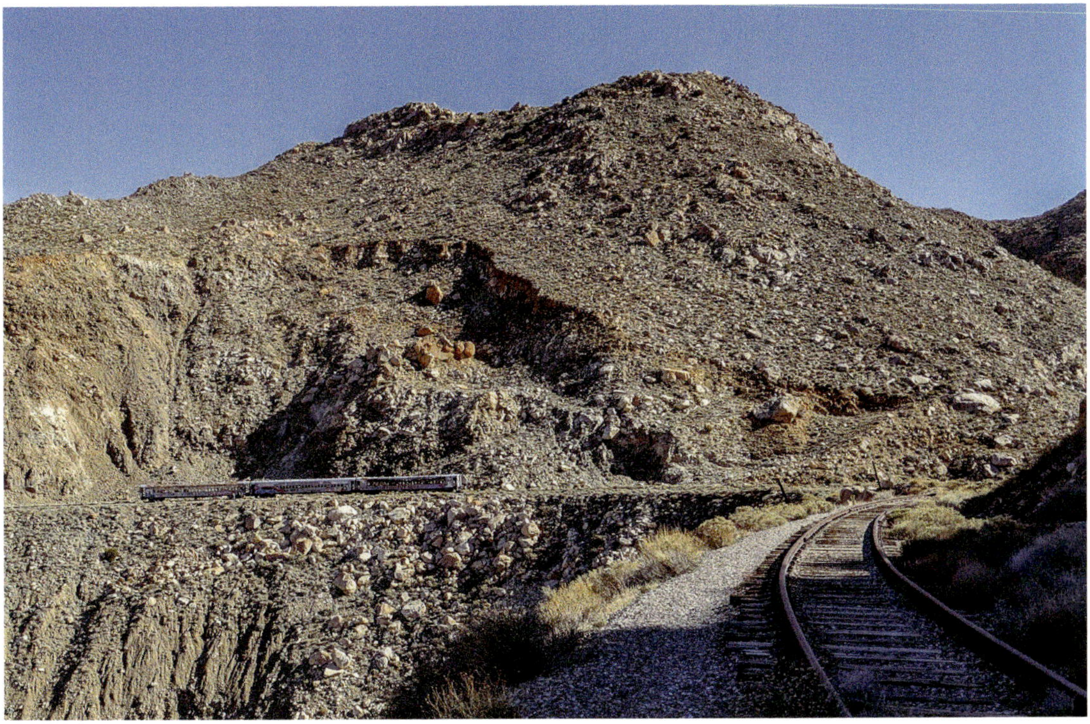

Coming up to another section of train cars.

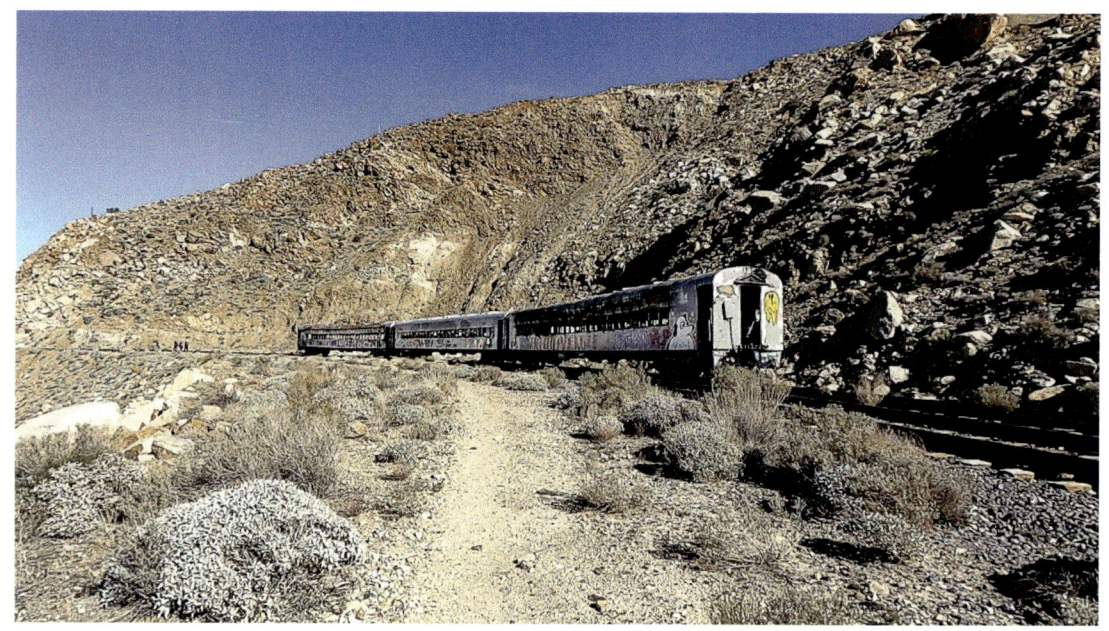

Three single-level passenger cars.

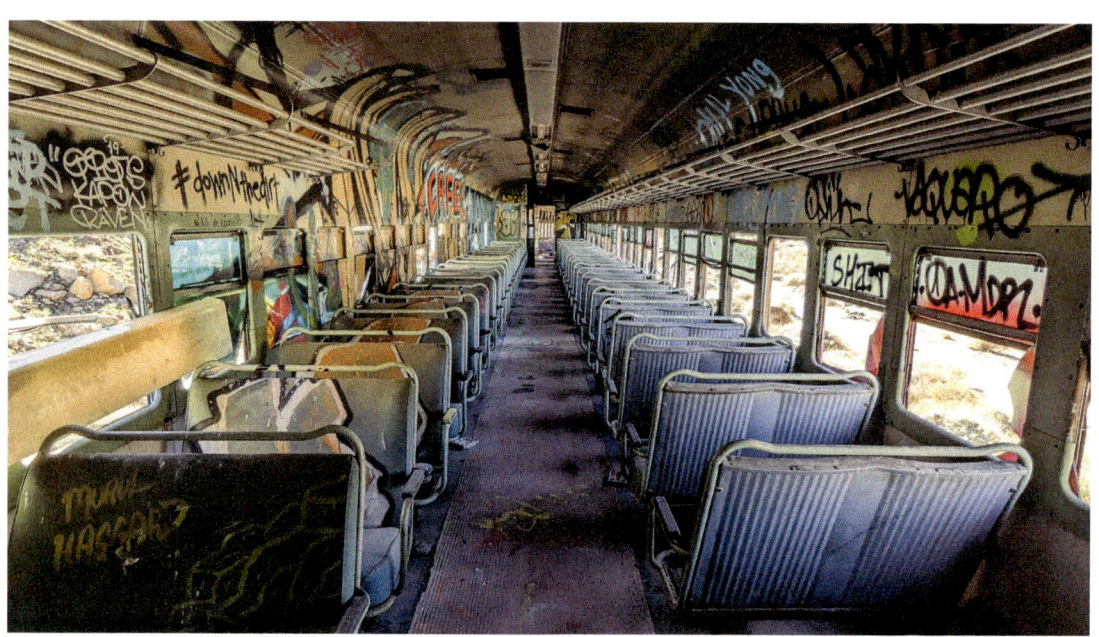

The interior of these passenger cars. I found labels in French, so this most likely came from Quebec, Canada.

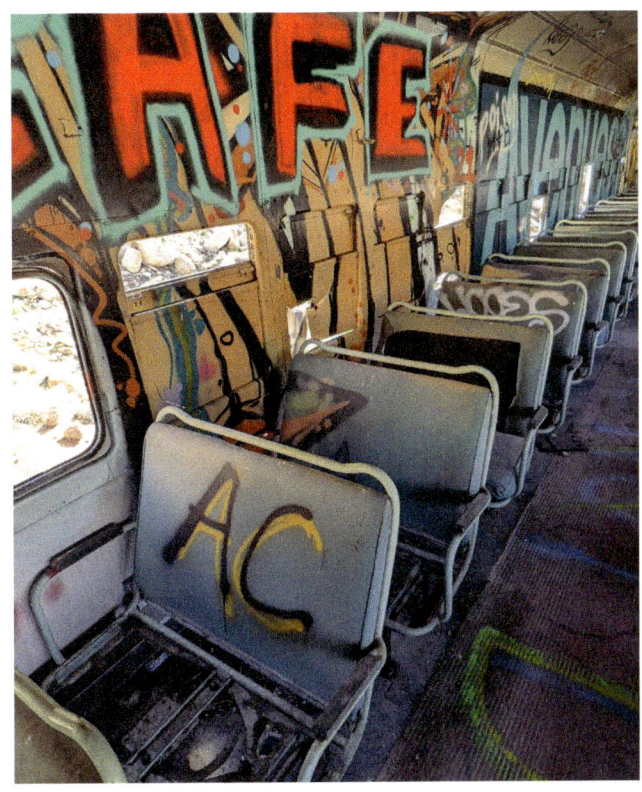

Passenger seats.

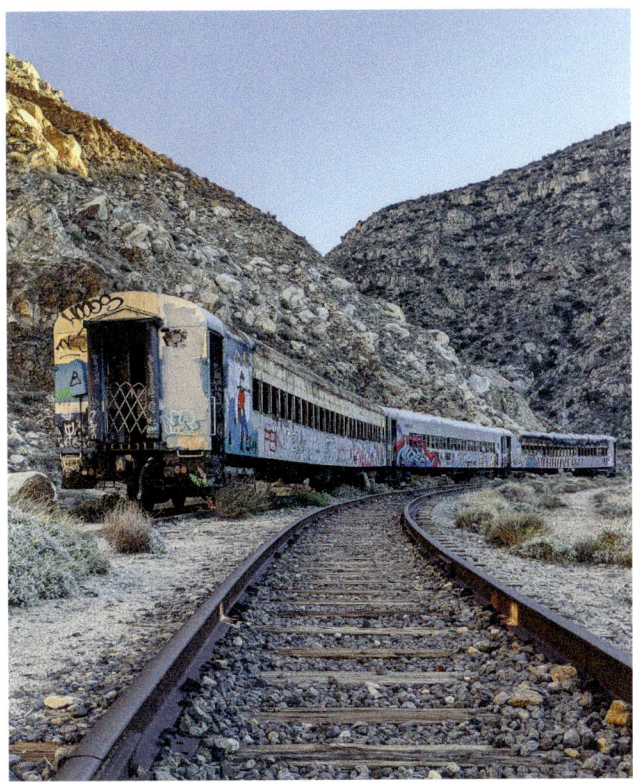

Parked long ago.

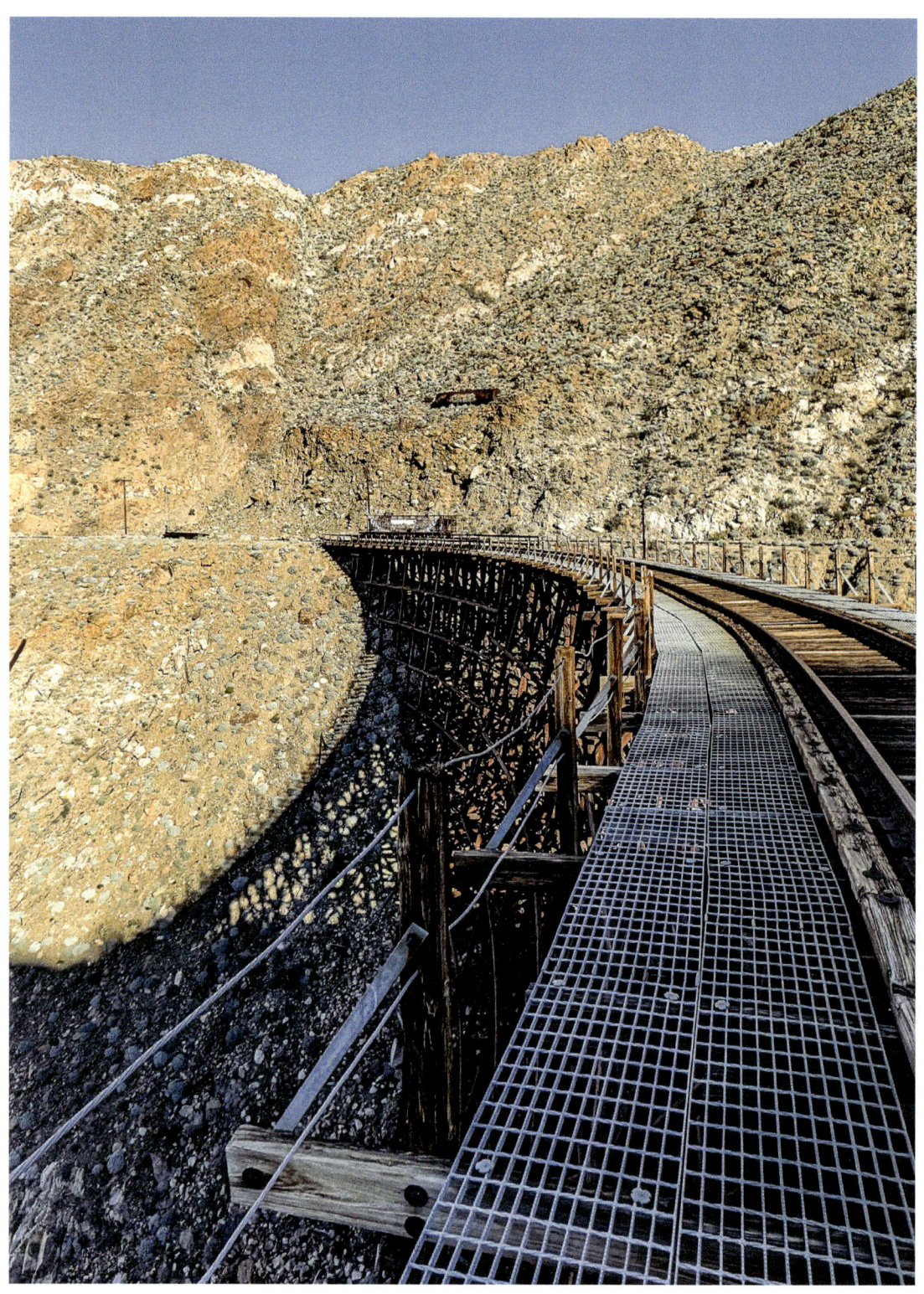

On top of the Goat Canyon trestle bridge. In the distance you can see the water car on the hill, which would have been used in case a fire broke out.

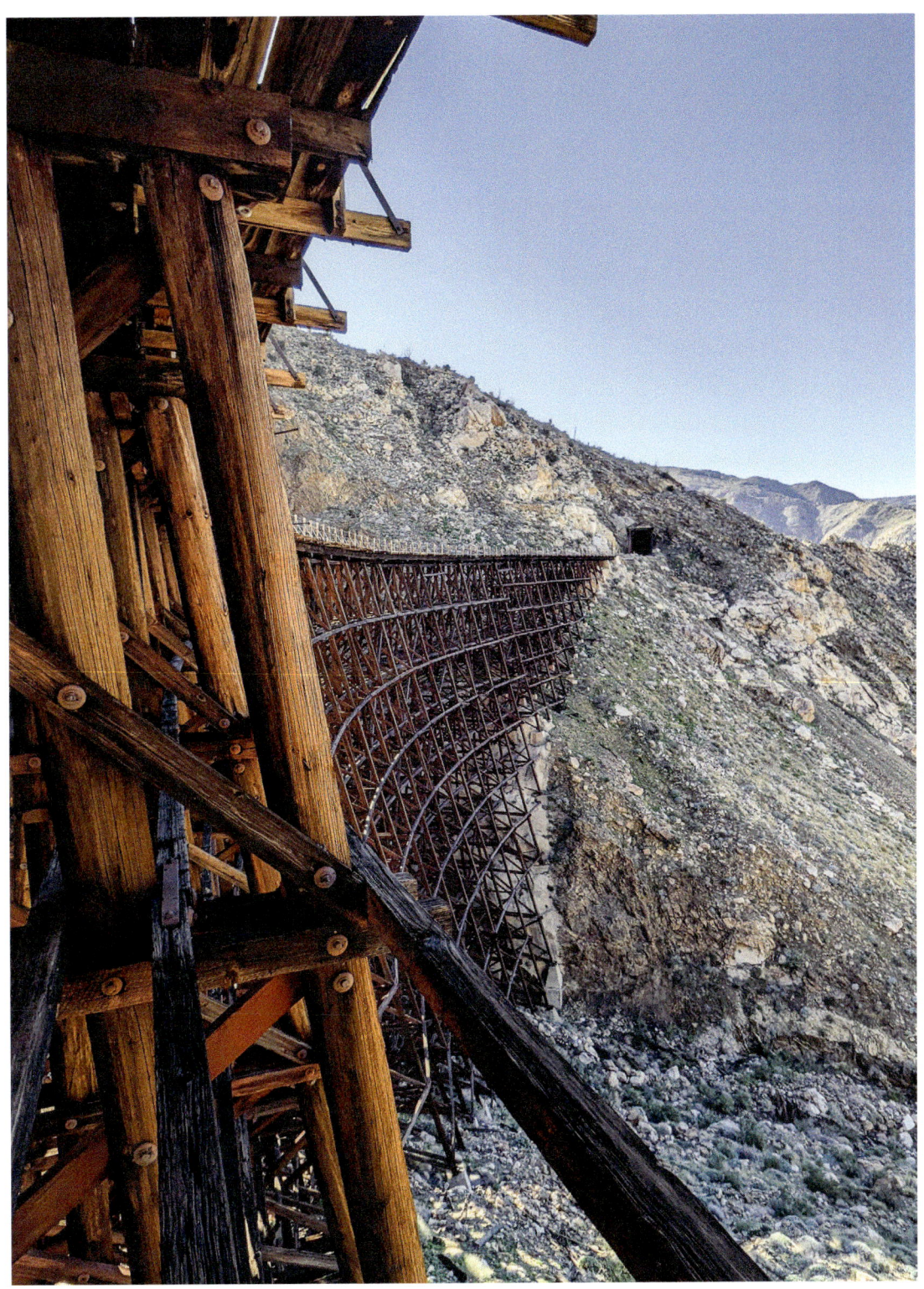

On the far end of the bridge, the underpass was accessible. Here you can see the framework of the bridge.

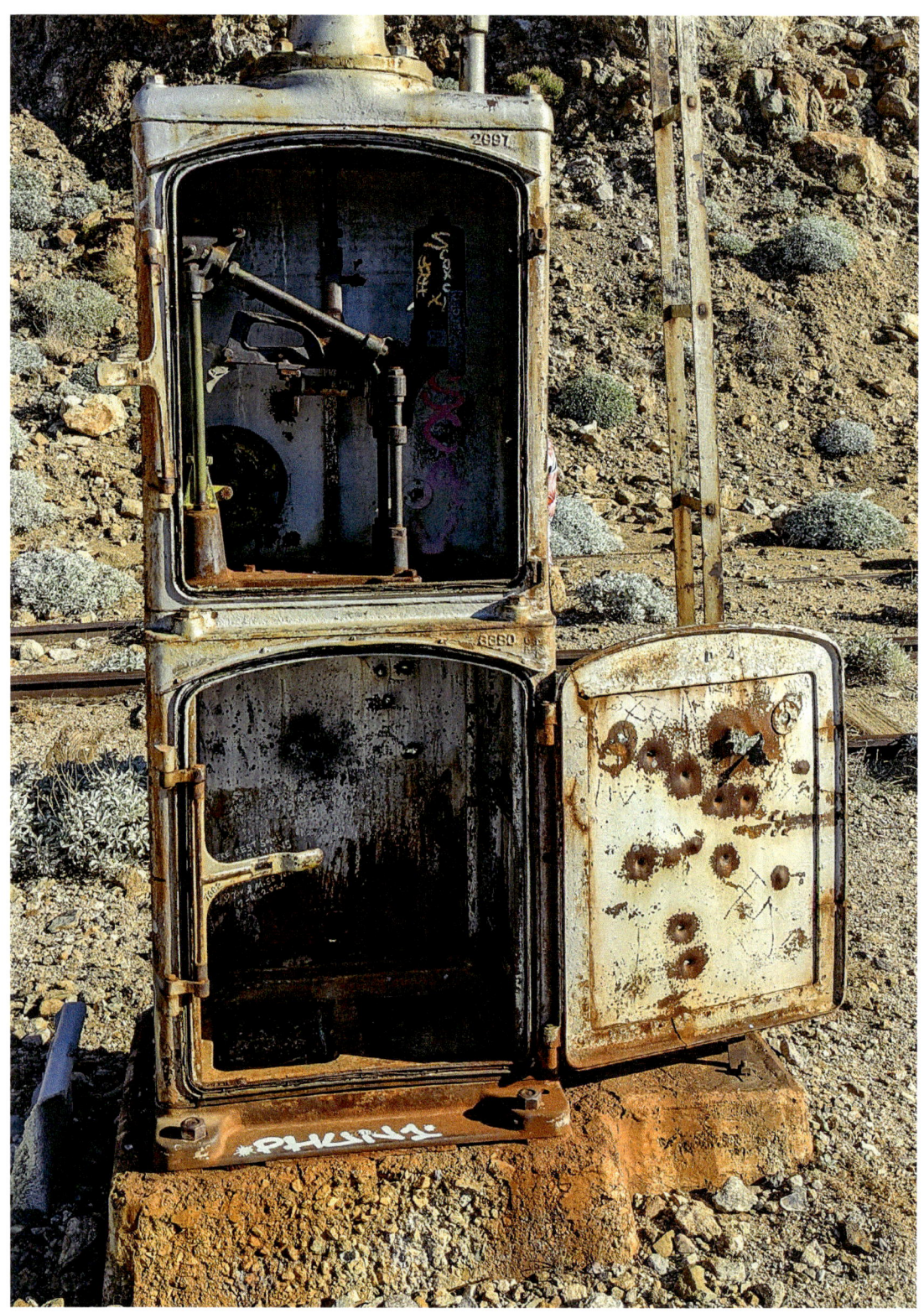

An old signal mast that most likely held electrical components which would operate a railroad signal light.

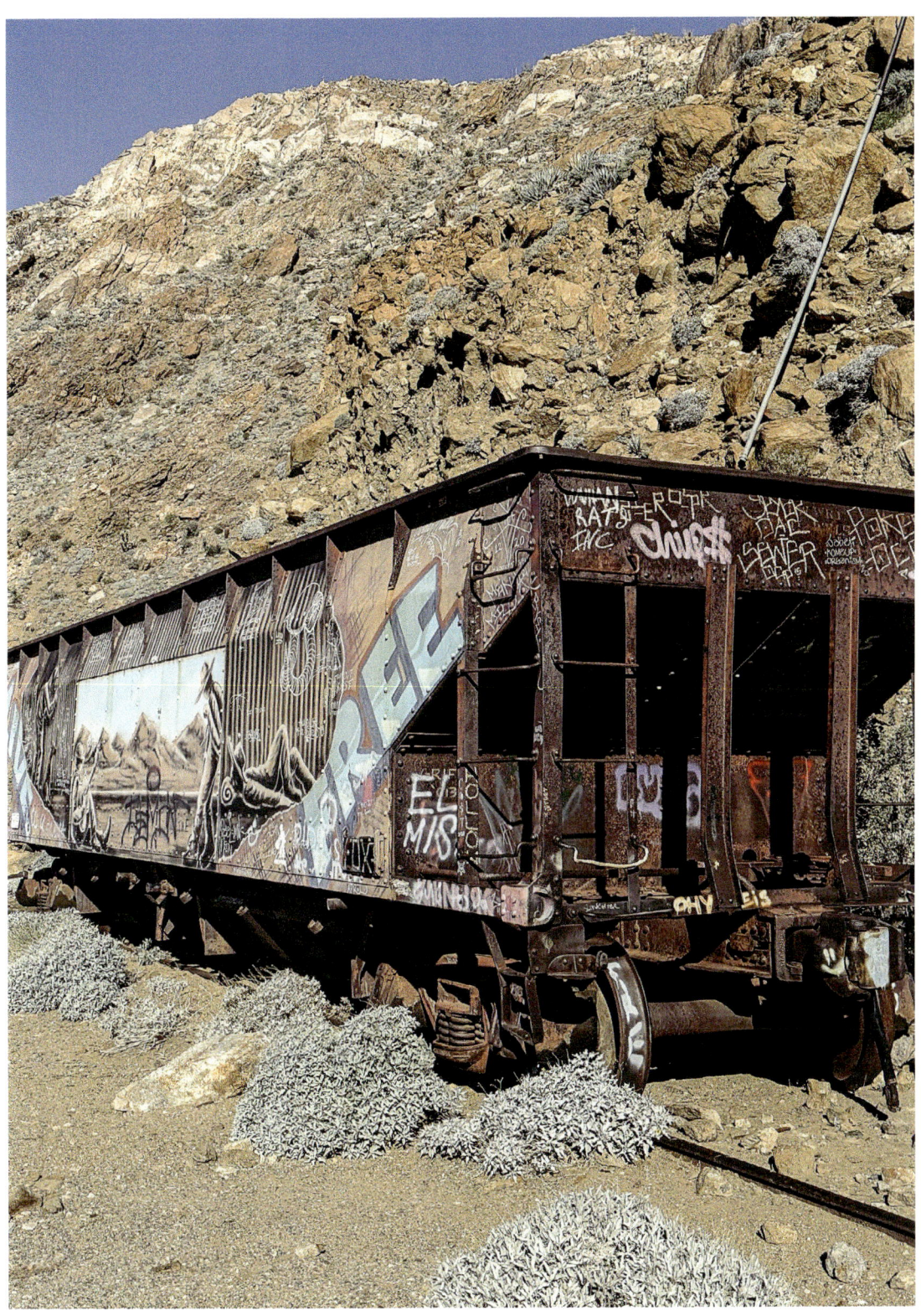

One of the only cargo cars found on the line.

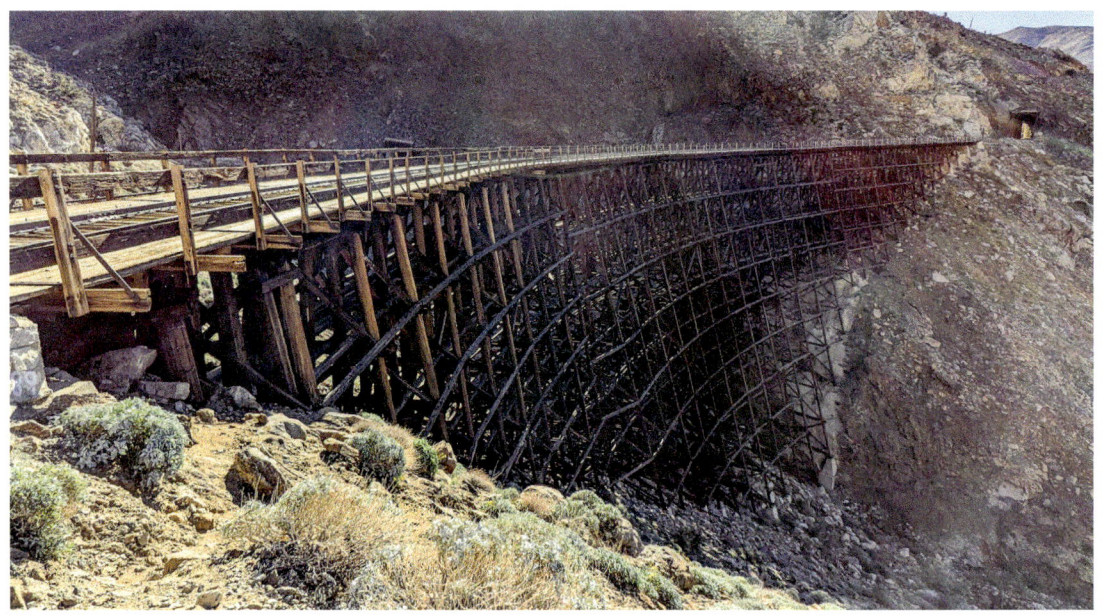

Standing at the edge of the Goat Canyon trestle bridge.

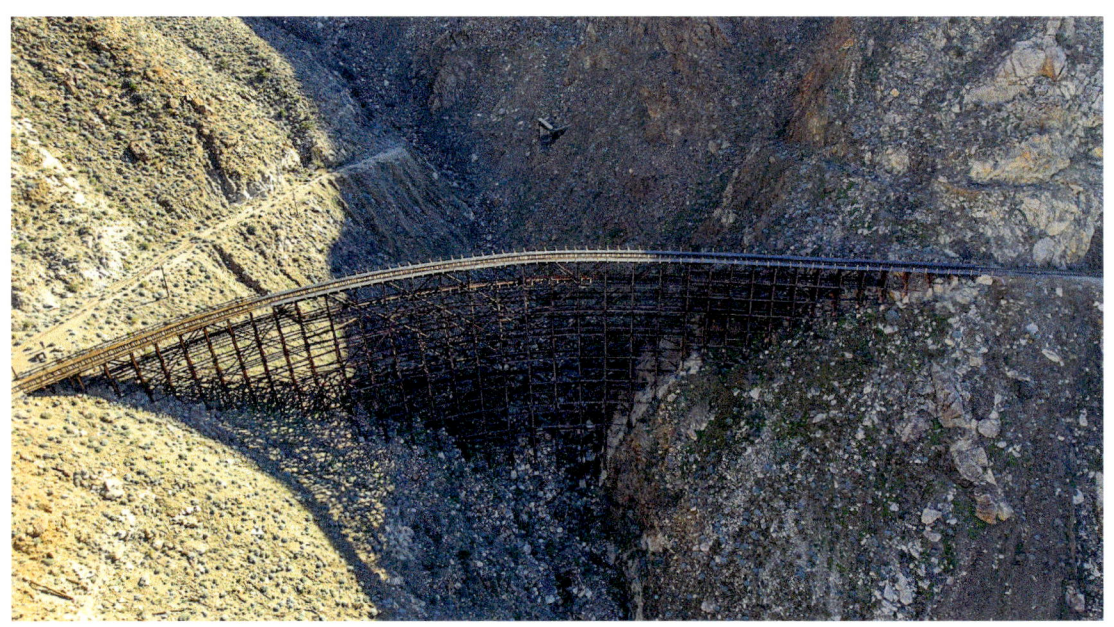

An aerial view of the Goat Canyon trestle bridge. If you look closely, you can see the old railroad line and the entrance to the collapsed tunnel, which prompted the construction of this bridge.

3

EAGLE MOUNTAIN MINE:
400 BUILDINGS LEFT BEHIND

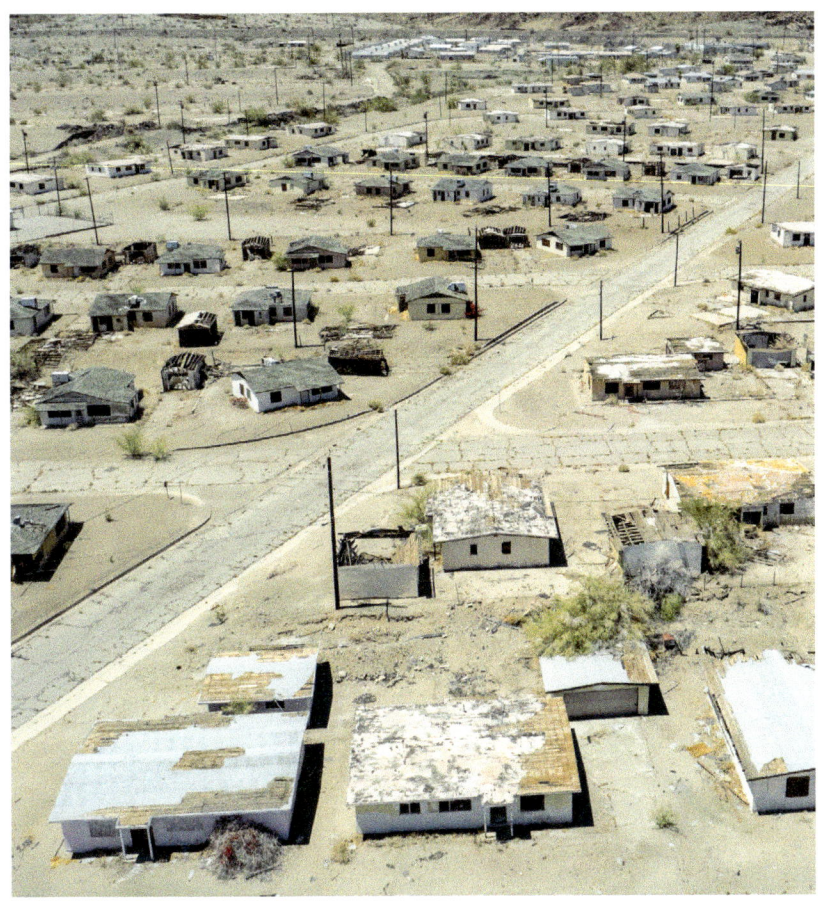

The remains of the town of Eagle Mountain, which was created for workers of the steel mine.

In the vast expanse of the California Desert, far removed from the bustling centers of civilization, lies the haunting legacy of Eagle Mountain. This once-thriving community, now an eerie ghost town, is a testament to the passage of time and the unpredictable tides of economic fortune. Stretching over 10,000 acres of desolate land, the remnants of Eagle Mountain bear witness to the rise and fall of a mining operation that once held the dreams of prosperity.

Perched on the edge of the mountains, at the far end of the town, stands the skeletal remains of a deserted steel mine. More than 400 dilapidated structures, now weathered and worn after four decades of abandonment, silently narrate the story of a community left to decay in the harsh embrace of the desert.

Eagle Mountain's story begins with the discovery of iron ore deposits in the mid-twentieth century. In 1948, the Kaiser Steel Corporation, recognizing the economic potential of these reserves, breathed life into the region, creating a thriving mining operation. The boom years saw the emergence of a vibrant town, complete with schools, stores, and houses lining wide, landscaped streets. At its peak, Eagle Mountain boasted a population of more than 4,000.

For several decades, the Eagle Mountain Mine played a crucial role in the steel industry, extracting iron ore that journeyed via a dedicated railroad to processing plants for refinement and transformation into steel products. However, the tides turned as market dynamics, environmental concerns, and global economic shifts influenced a decrease in the demand for iron ore. Faced with increased competition and evolving technologies, the Kaiser Steel Corporation experienced a decline in production and financial hardships.

By the 1980s, the Eagle Mountain Mine faced its demise, echoing the fate of the town itself. Structures were dismantled, and the once-thriving community morphed into a ghost town. Today, the only active building is a school catering to residents of Desert Center, a town located 12 miles away.

Efforts to repurpose Eagle Mountain have been met with mixed success. In 1986, a glimmer of revival appeared when the California Department of Corrections proposed the establishment of a privately operated prison for low-risk inmates. The Eagle Mountain Community Correctional Facility emerged in 1988, but its journey was fraught with challenges. Budgetary issues and a fatal riot led to the facility's closure in December 2003. The desolate landscape, however, found a second life as a cinematic backdrop for movies like *The Island* (2005), *Battle of Los Angeles* (2011), and *Tenet* (2020), as well as the popular television show *Top Gear USA* which has filmed at Eagle Mountain on several occasions.

After lingering on the market for over forty years, on April 17, 2023, the land and mining site found a new owner in California-based Ecology Mountain Holdings. A transaction valued at $22.5 million marked the beginning of a new chapter for Eagle Mountain, yet the plans of the new owners remain unclear. As the sun sets over the deserted landscape, the future of Eagle Mountain remains uncertain.

The Eagle Mountain property is under heavy surveillance, with multiple security guards working twenty-four hours a day. When I visited the property, I was not allowed to enter, but the guards did allow me to fly a drone.

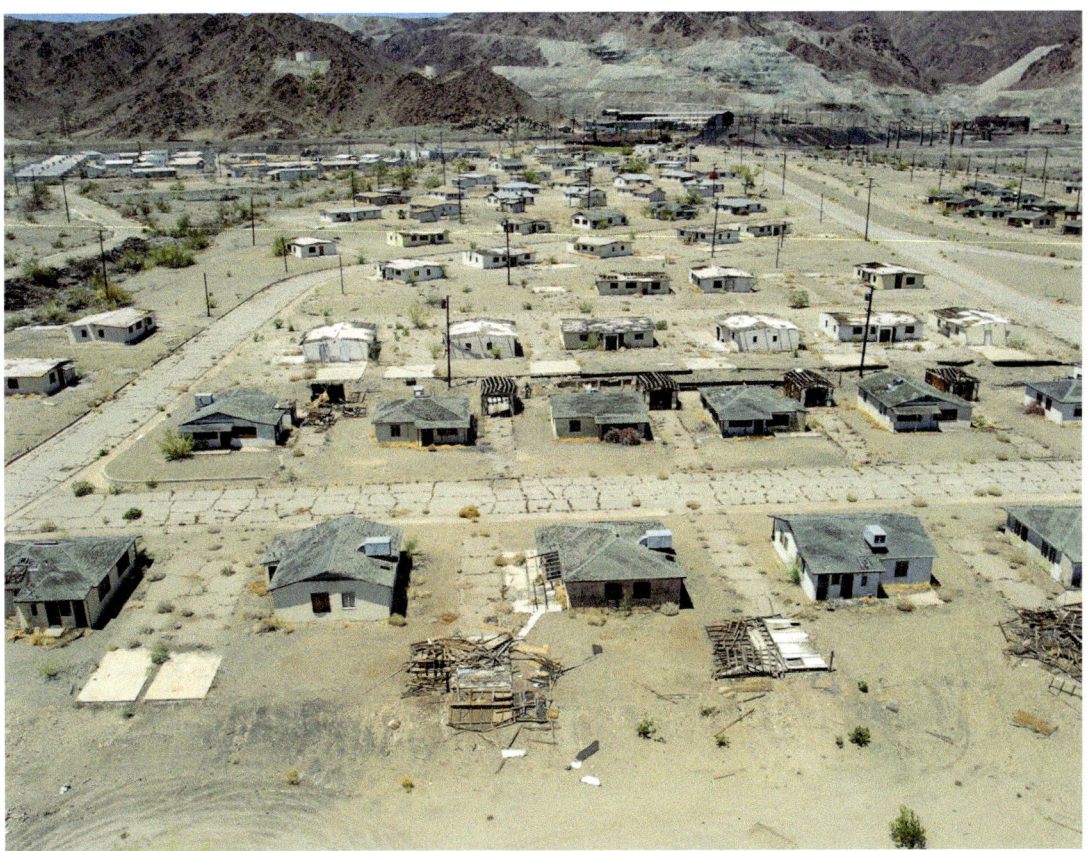

The streets of the town can be seen here, with the mine in the distant background. Most of the houses are still standing, however, the garages have mostly fallen down. You can see air-conditioning units that are still on the roofs of several houses. A lot of the power line poles are also still standing.

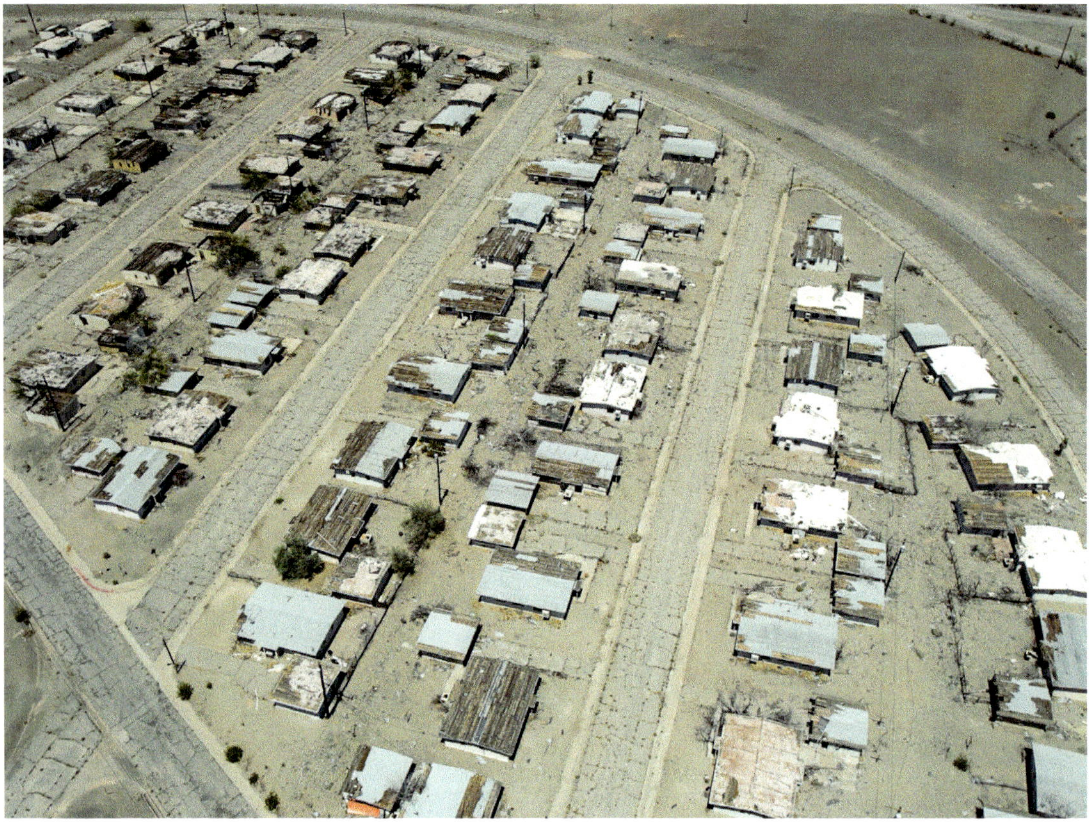

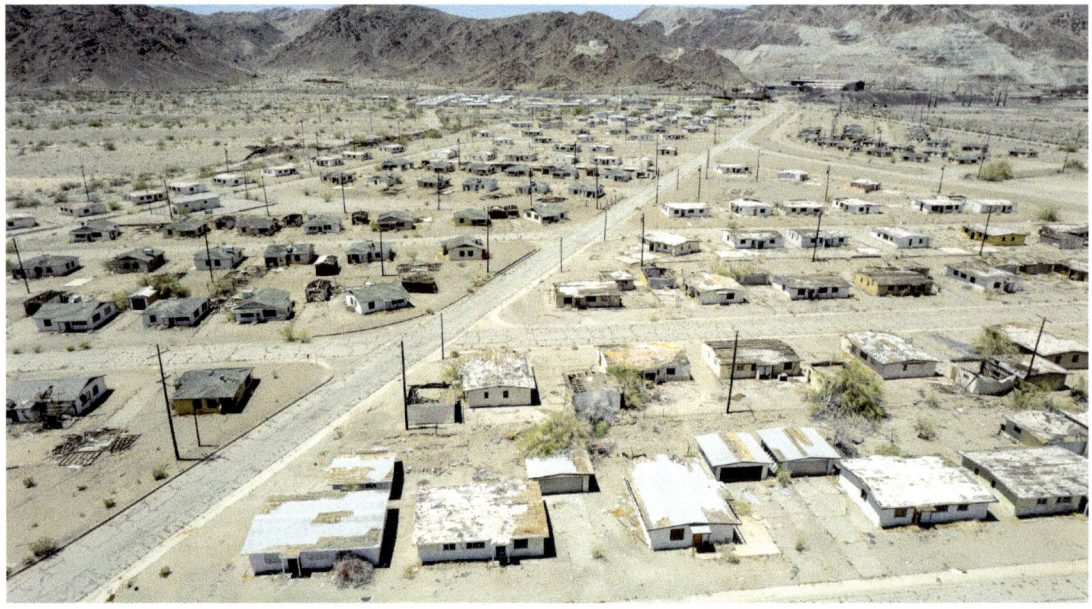

This aerial perspective shows another residential area, where some of the houses have fenced in backyards. You can see a main street at the top of the photo, which would lead directly to the mine.

Hundreds of houses remain.

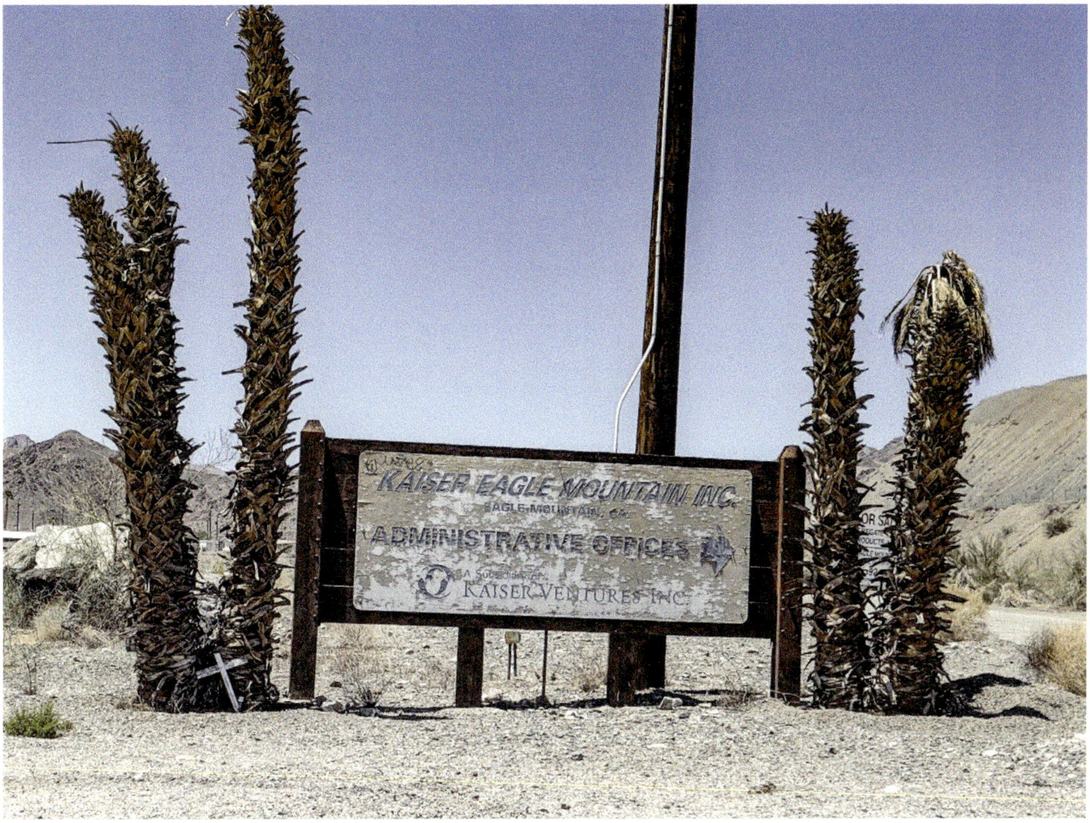

Above: A sign at the entrance, right by the security gate.

Right: In this image, you can see several areas where houses have been demolished, including a whole subdivision in the upper left corner of the photo. The workforce was very big at one time.

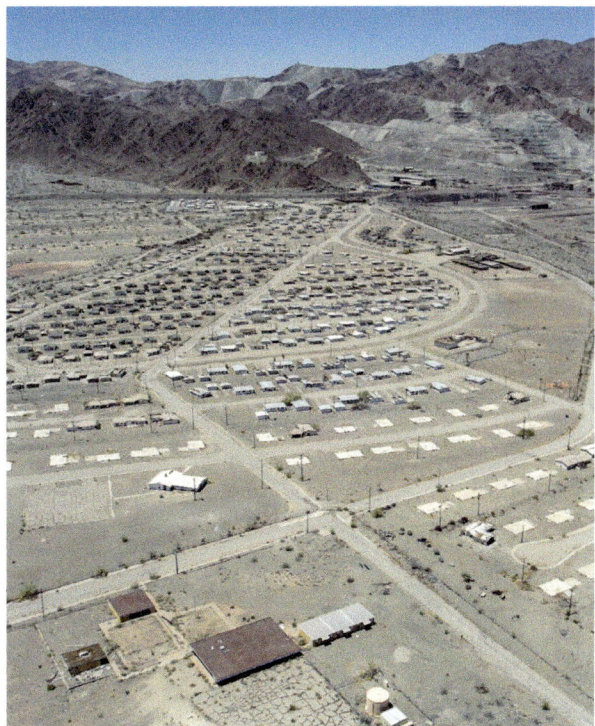

4

DESERT CENTER: THE BIRTHPLACE OF MODERN HEALTHCARE

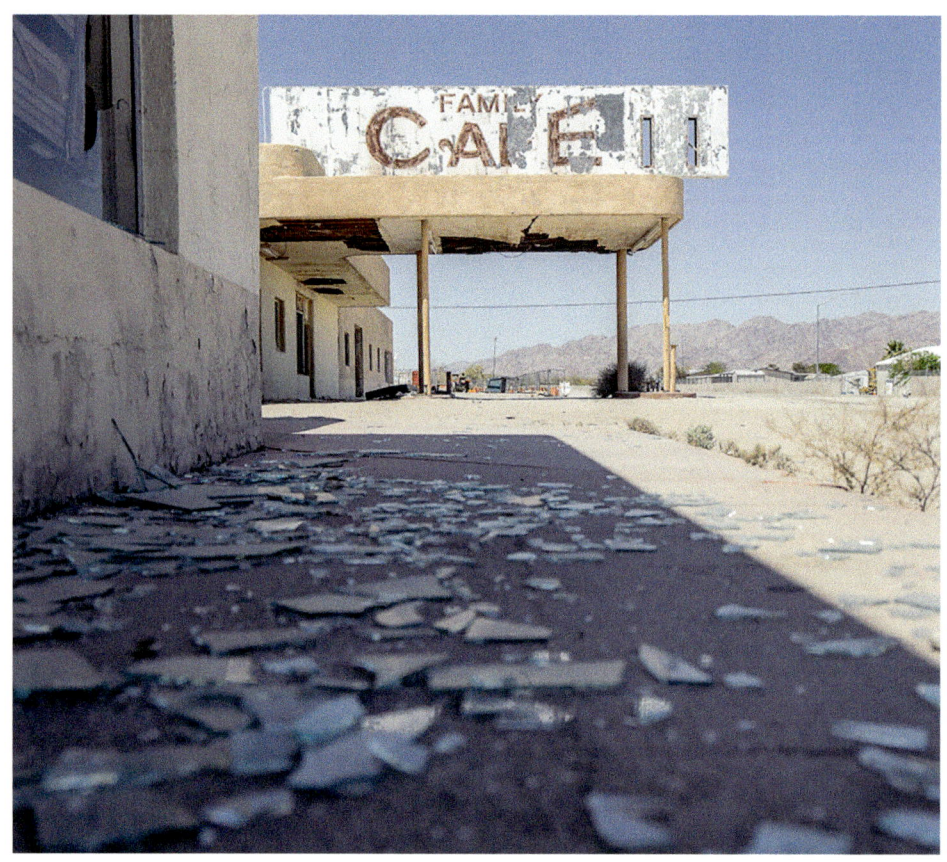

The family café at Desert Center.

Some 12 miles away from Eagle Mountain lies the almost forgotten town of Desert Center, a settlement with roots dating back to its founding in 1921. Once a bustling oasis along the route from Los Angeles to Phoenix, Desert Center thrived as a crucial stop for travelers and those conducting business at the Eagle Mountain mine. The town's historical landscape, now frozen in time, unveils a narrative of prosperity and subsequent abandonment.

In its heyday, Desert Center boasted several gas stations, a market, café, hotel, and a modest elementary school. A pivotal point in the town's history was its service to the workers of the Colorado River Aqueduct, which redirected water from Lake Havasu across the Mojave Desert to Southern California cities. In the absence of medical services within a 50-mile radius, a small clinic was established in Desert Center, staffed by a doctor. However, collecting payment for medical bills from the workforce proved to be a challenge.

Enter Henry J. Kaiser, the visionary owner of the Eagle Mountain Mine. Kaiser, along with the contractor overseeing the aqueduct's construction through Desert Center, devised a groundbreaking solution. They deducted a nickel a day from each worker's paycheck to prepay for future medical treatments, and an additional nickel covered their family members. This pioneering initiative laid the foundation for Kaiser Permanente, now one of the world's largest healthcare systems, with its roots deeply embedded in the sands of Desert Center.

The town's significance continued during the 1940s when Desert Center played host to an 18,000-square-mile military base. Camp Desert Center and the Desert Center Army Airfield became instrumental in General S. Patton's efforts to train troops for combat in the North African Theatre during World War II. However, with the war's conclusion, the base fell silent, a testament to the transient nature of military presence.

In the present day, Desert Center stands as a quiet outpost with a handful of residents, and the sole business in operation is a U.S. Post Office. The surrounding landscape has evolved into a hub of renewable energy, with vast expanses of solar panels generating electricity for Southern California cities.

Desert Center stands as a testament to the ever-changing tapestry of time. The whispers of a once-thriving town and its pivotal role in the creation of a healthcare giant reverberate through the quiet streets, casting Desert Center as a silent witness to the ebb and flow of human endeavors in the heart of the California Desert.

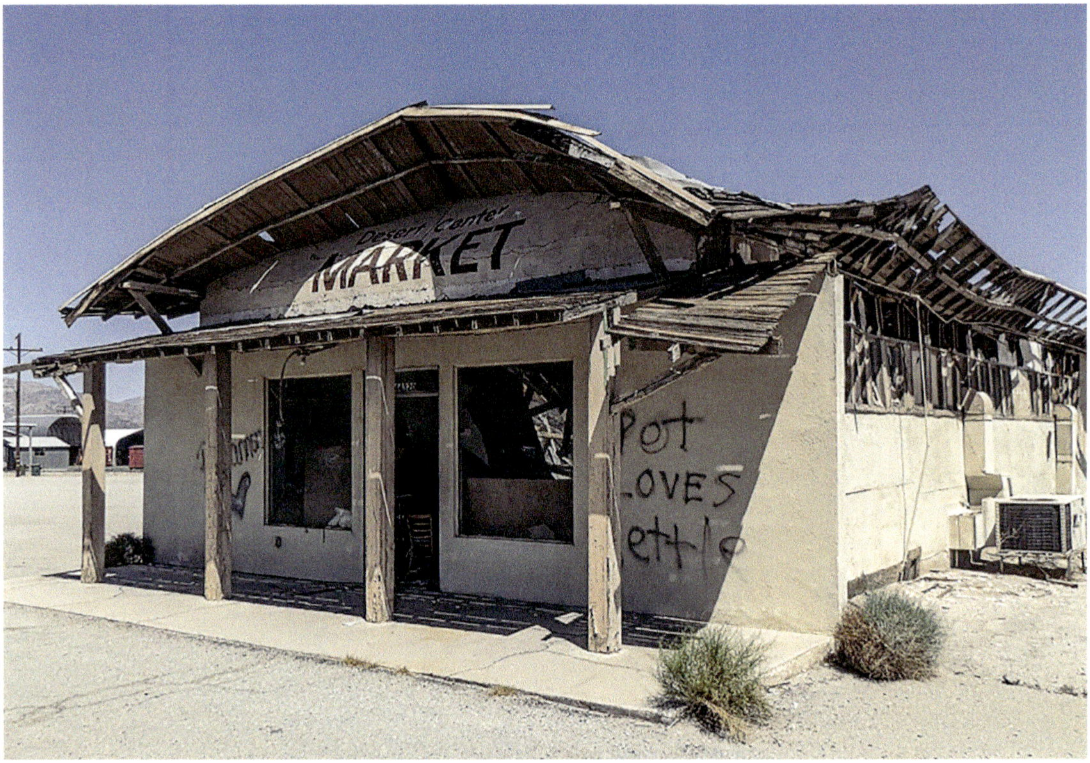

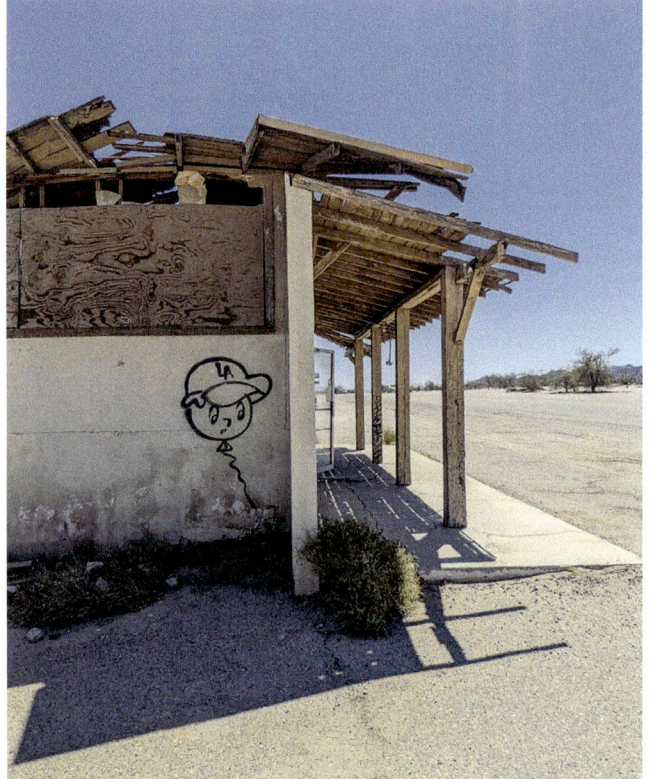

Above: Desert Center Market, a small grocery store, with the roof collapsing in on itself.

Left: The side of Desert Center Market, looking down main street.

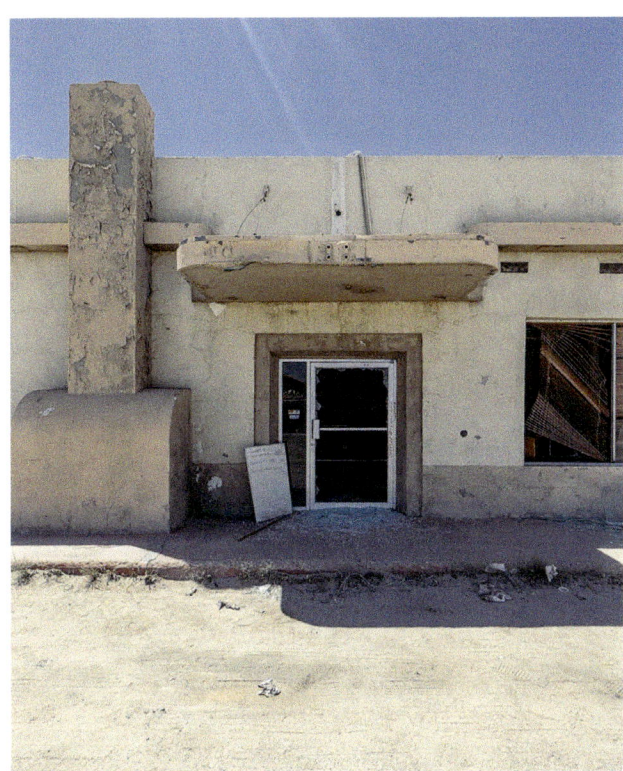

Right: Entrance to the café.

Below: The café with boarded windows and what would have been gas pumps at one time.

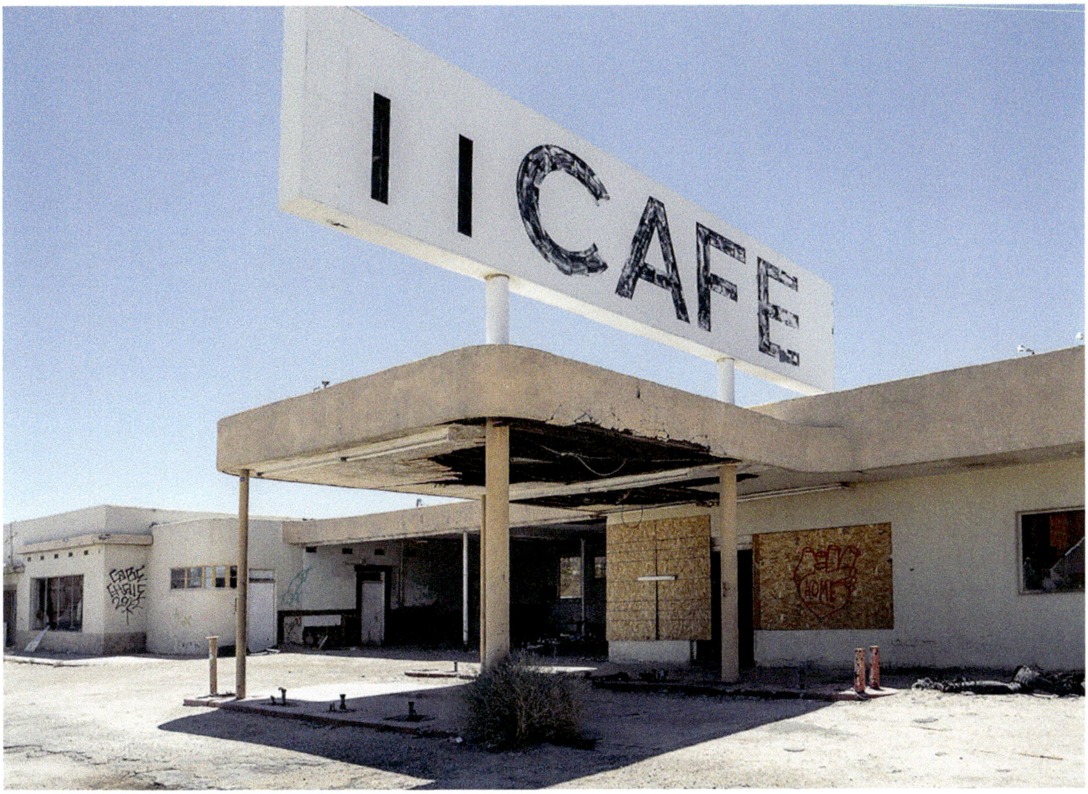

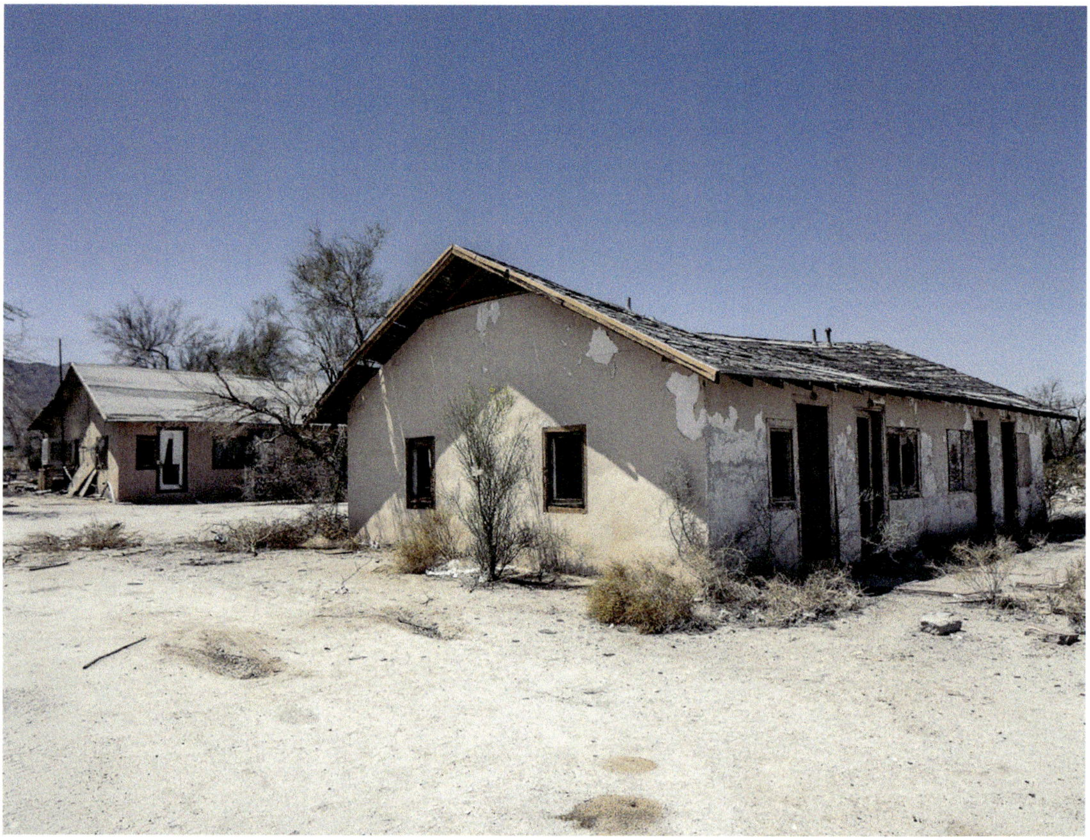

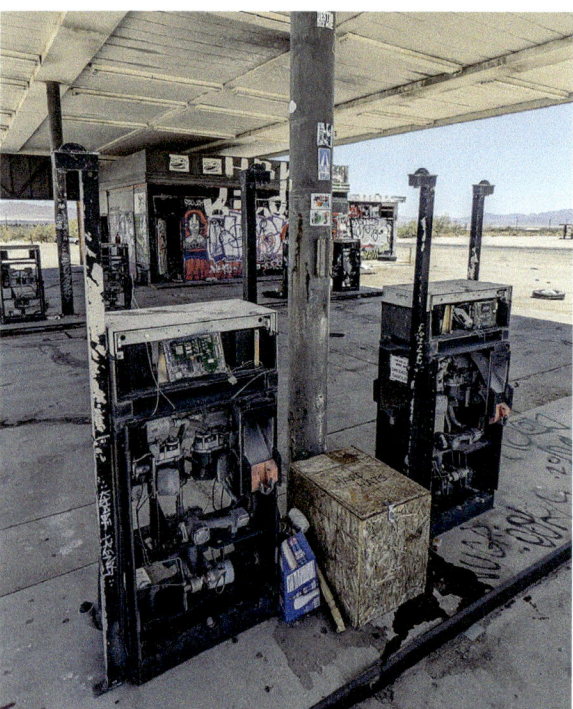

Above: These buildings were used as rooms in a motel at one point, but it looks like more recently they have been used as apartments before becoming abandoned.

Left: Gas pumps at the more modern abandoned gas station.

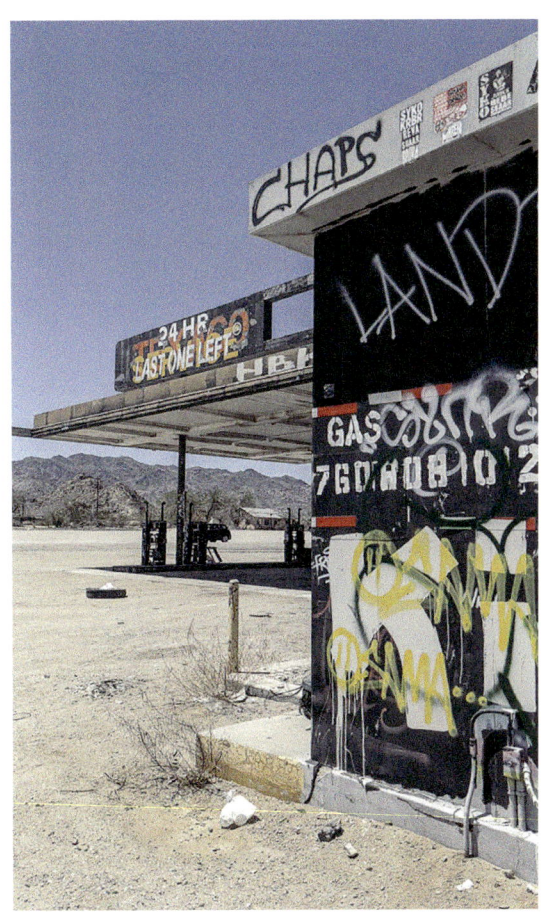

Gas station looking onto main
street and the freeway.

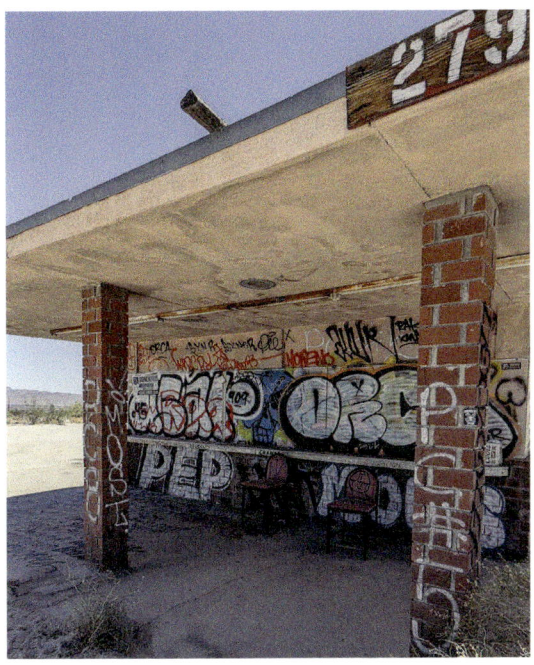

Remains of a counter serve
restaurant/ice cream shop.

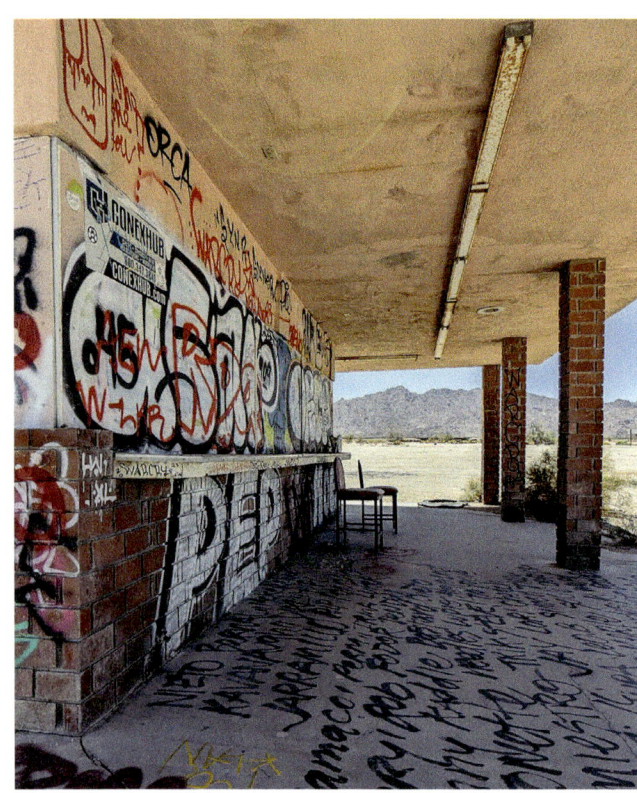

Left: Service counter.

Below: The Desert Center Elementary School.

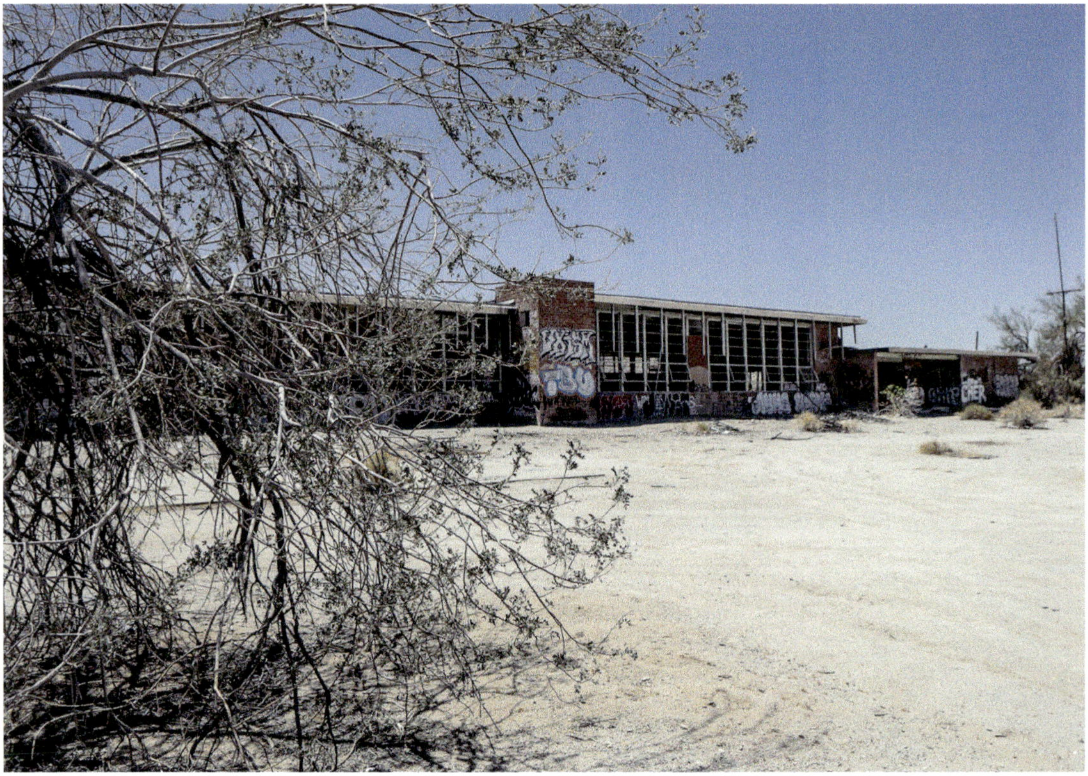

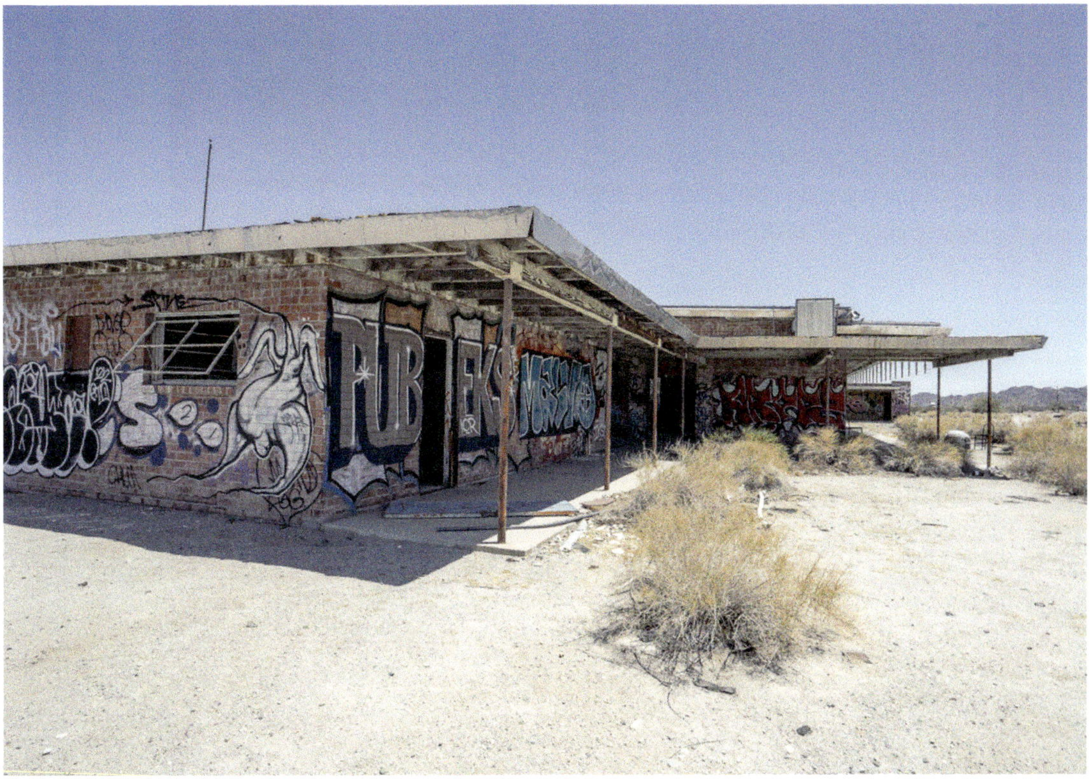

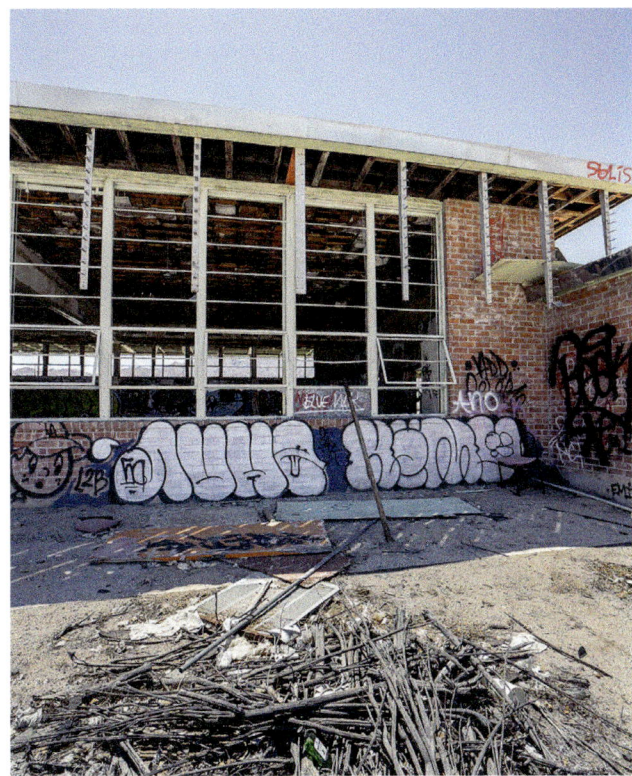

Above: This school closed in 1989, when remaining students started to attend the school at Eagle Mountain.

Right: All of the glass has been broken out.

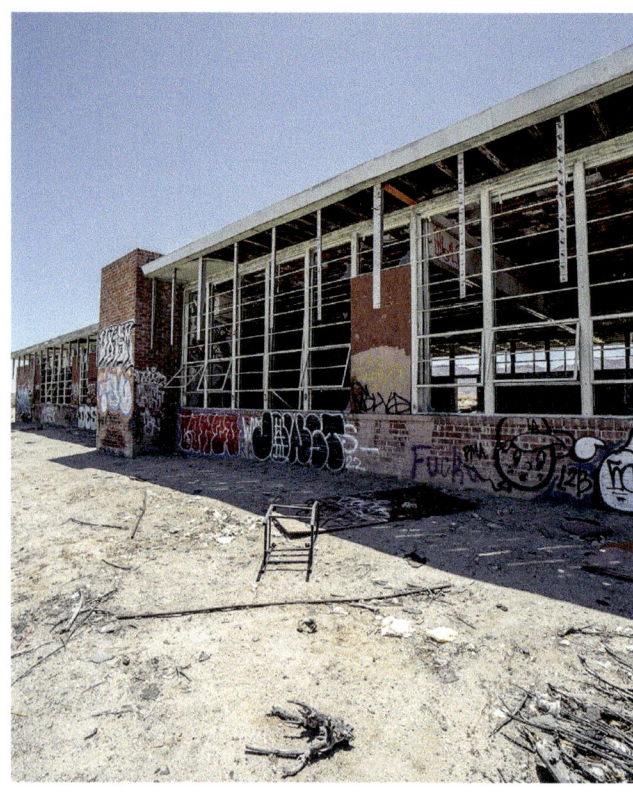

A lone chair lays outside.

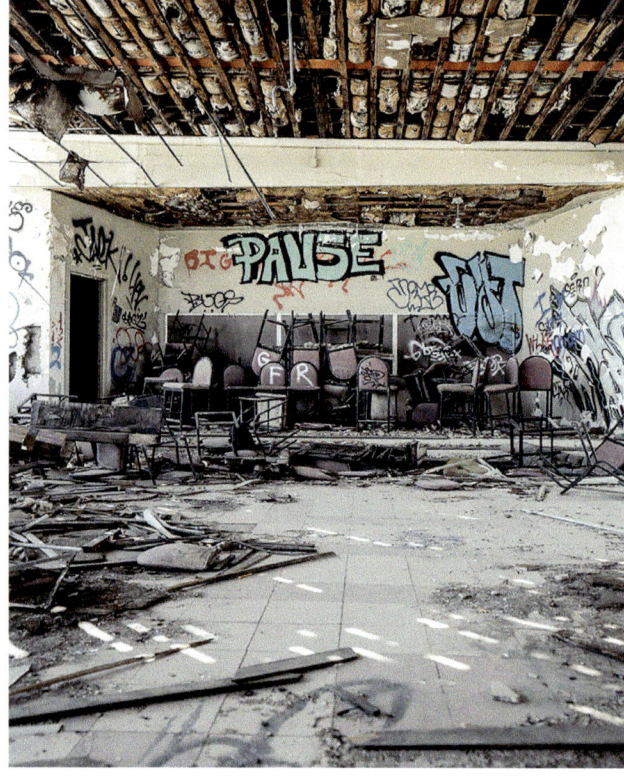

Inside one of the main rooms, with a stage at the far end of the room. This room was most likely used as a cafeteria.

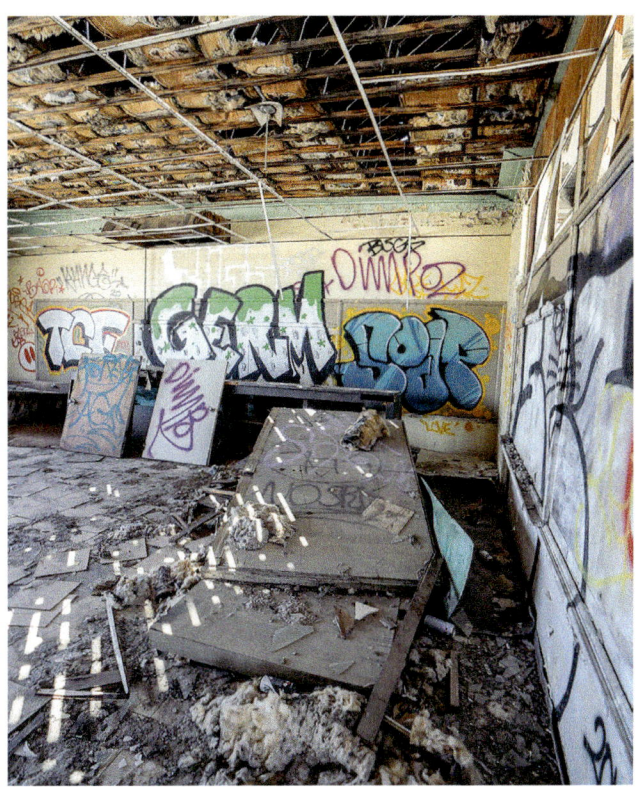

Chalkboards now covered with graffiti.

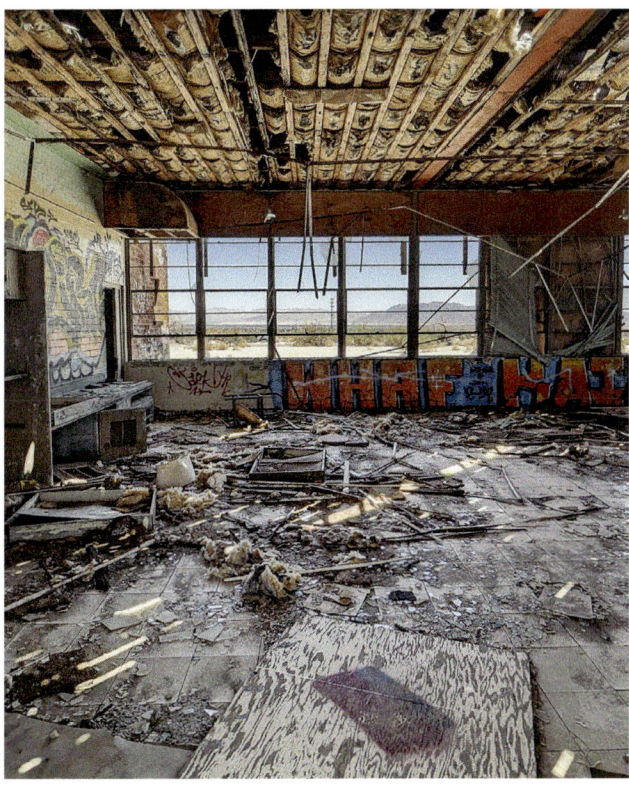

The insulation in the celling is starting to fall.

5

LAKE DOLORES: AMERICA'S FIRST WATERPARK

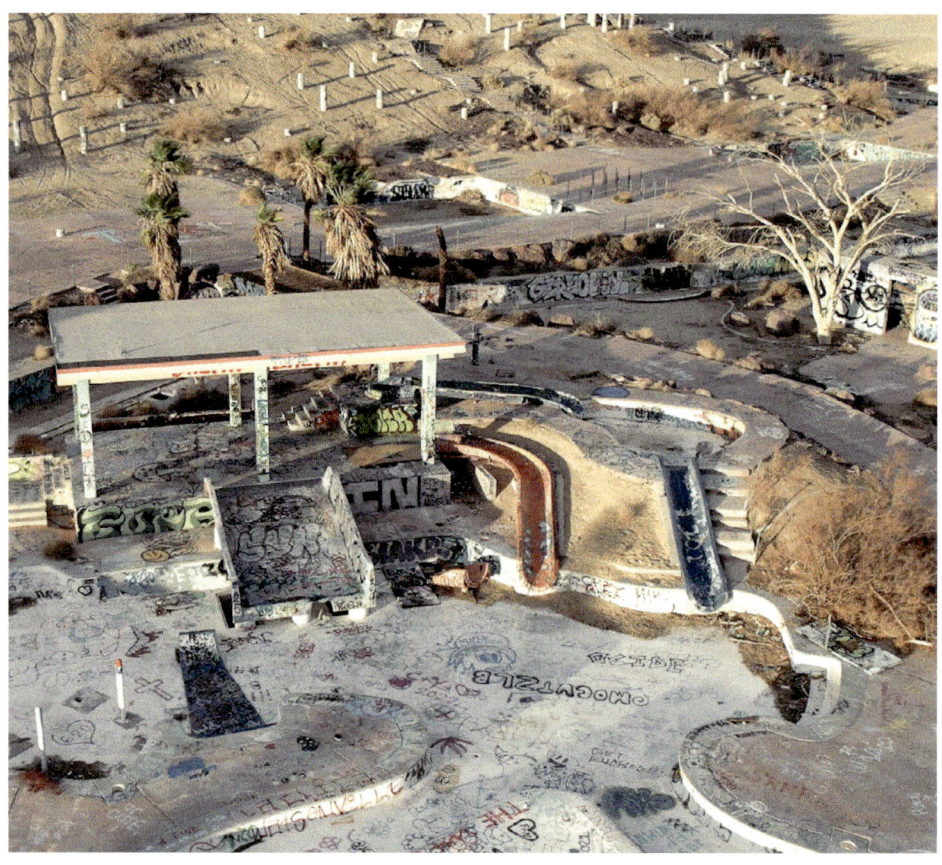

Aerial perspective of Lake Dolores Water Park ruins.

Nestled in the sun-soaked expanses of the Mojave Desert, Lake Dolores Waterpark emerged as a testament to the vision of local entrepreneur Bob Byers. Originally conceived as a private retreat for Byers' immediate family, the waterpark bore the name of his beloved wife, Dolores. Spanning an impressive 273 acres, the park's centerpiece was a man-made body of water, generously fed by pumping water up from the Mojave aquifer.

In the year 1962, Byers expanded his vision by constructing an adjoining camp-ground, opening the gates of Lake Dolores Waterpark to the public. The early attractions were a departure from the modern waterpark experience, showcasing a unique blend of thrills and simplicity that defined an era. Eight colossal 150-foot steel water slides adorned a man-made hill, each slide offering an exhilarating ride on "floaties," propelling riders across the lagoon at the slide's conclusion.

Adding to the eclectic mix were two V-shaped waterslides that dared riders to stand tall as they plunged 15 feet into the refreshing waters of Lake Dolores. The park's daring spirit also manifested in the "Zip-Cord" ride, where riders hung from a handheld device, soaring over 200 feet before coming to a dramatic halt, suspended about 20 feet above the lagoon. A 20-foot-high platform played host to high diving boards and trapeze-like swings, embodying an era where safety regulations took a backseat to the pursuit of unbridled fun.

Lake Dolores Waterpark witnessed its peak in attendance during the early 1970s through the mid-1980s, captivating the hearts of thrill-seekers with its one-of-a-kind attractions. However, the ensuing years were marked by a series of closures and rebranding efforts.

Byers sold the park in the early 1990's and Terry Christensen assumed ownership, introducing a fresh wave of attractions and entertainment, all inspired by the vibrant themes of 1950s and 1960s rock and roll music.

On the auspicious reopening date of July 4, 1998, the park underwent a name change, adopting the fitting moniker of Rock-A-Hoola. However, the trajectory of the park's fortunes took a downturn in the subsequent years. The infusion of newer rides and entertainment styles incurred substantial financial losses for the new owners. In 1999, an unfortunate incident added to the park's challenges when an employee, navigating a slide after operating hours, suffered serious injuries due to an inadequately deep catching water pool. In the aftermath of this incident, a lawsuit ensued, resulting in a legal settlement that exceeded $4 million being awarded to the injured employee. The property was closed shortly after.

The group reopened the park under the name Discovery Waterpark in 2002. This revitalization attempt was short-lived, as the park closed permanently in the summer of 2004.

Today, the remnants of Lake Dolores Waterpark stand as a nostalgic testament to a bygone era, a place where the carefree spirit of adventure and the refreshing embrace of water in an arid landscape created enduring memories for generations.

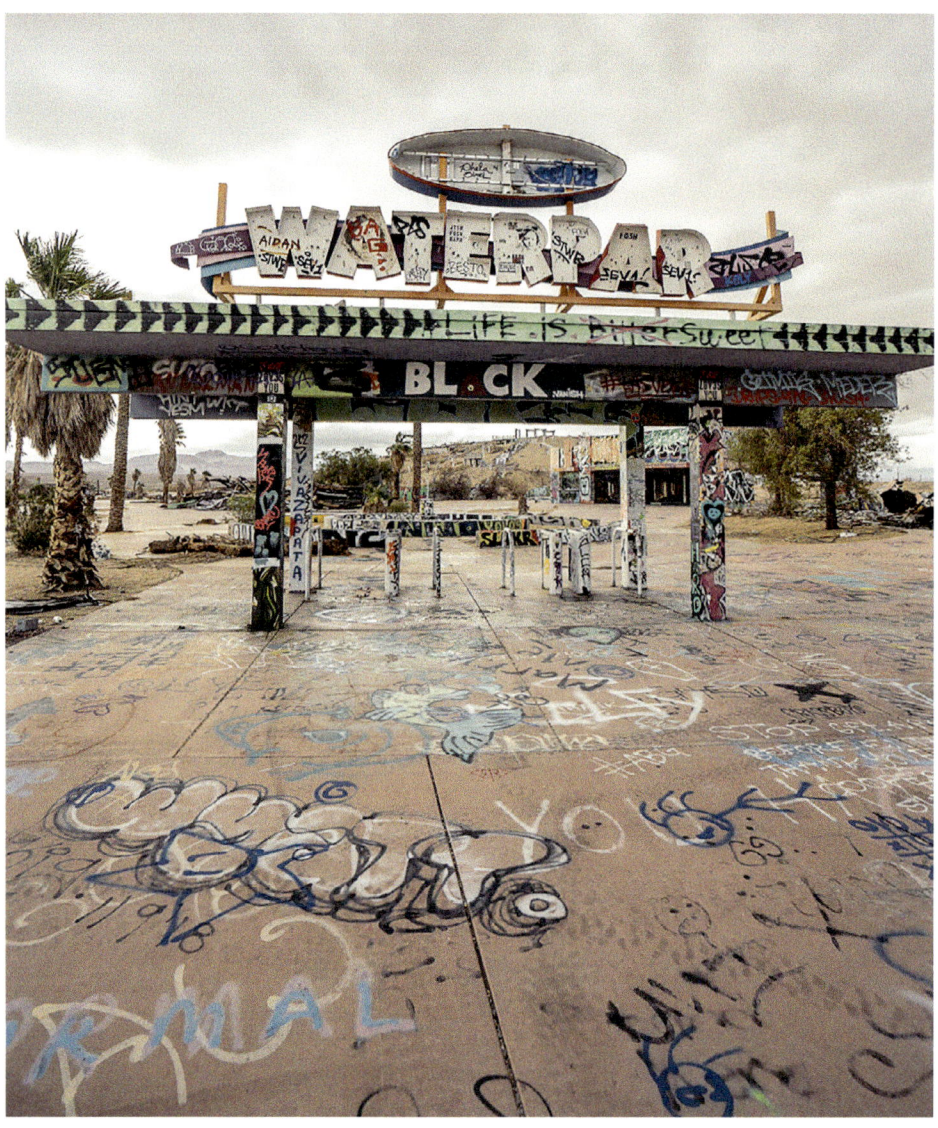

The main entrance to the waterpark.

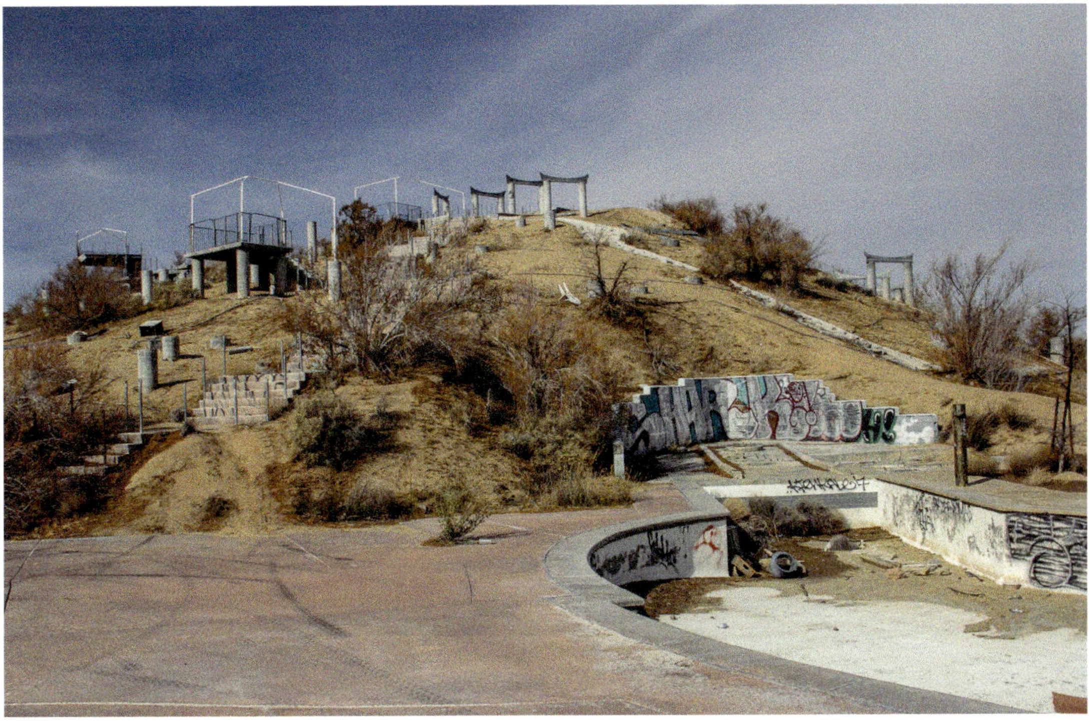

Looking up the man-made hill where the larger slides would have been. The slides have been removed, but the supports remain. You can also see one of the pools where riders would have come out of the slides.

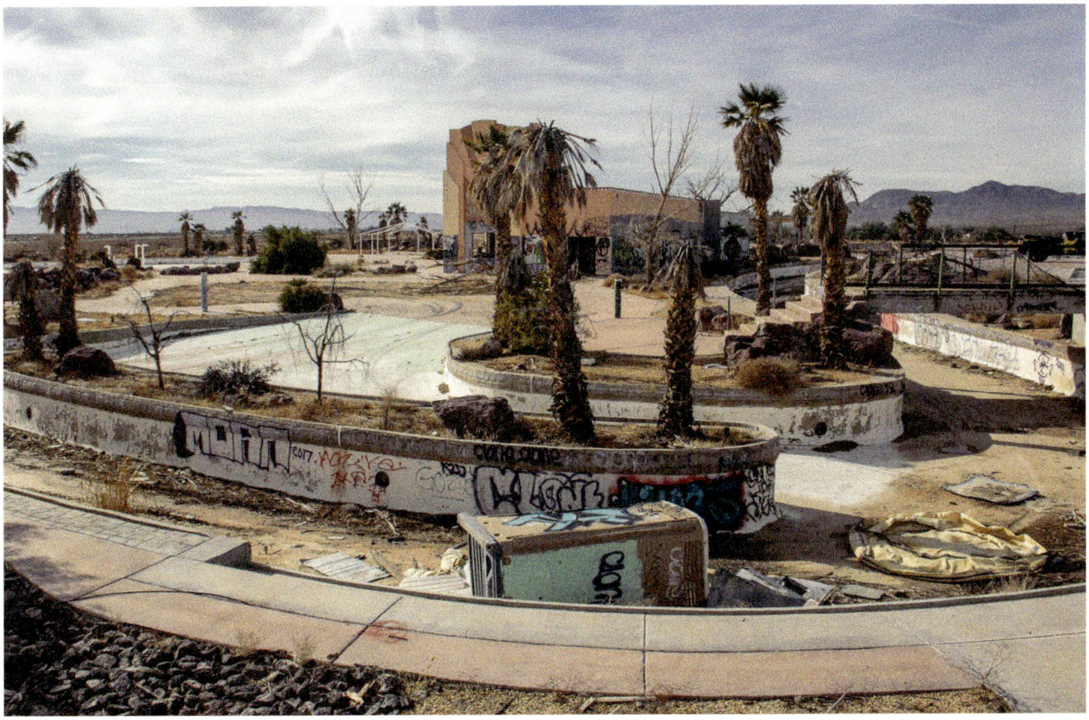

One of the entrances to the lazy river, with a bridge to allow people to access the center island.

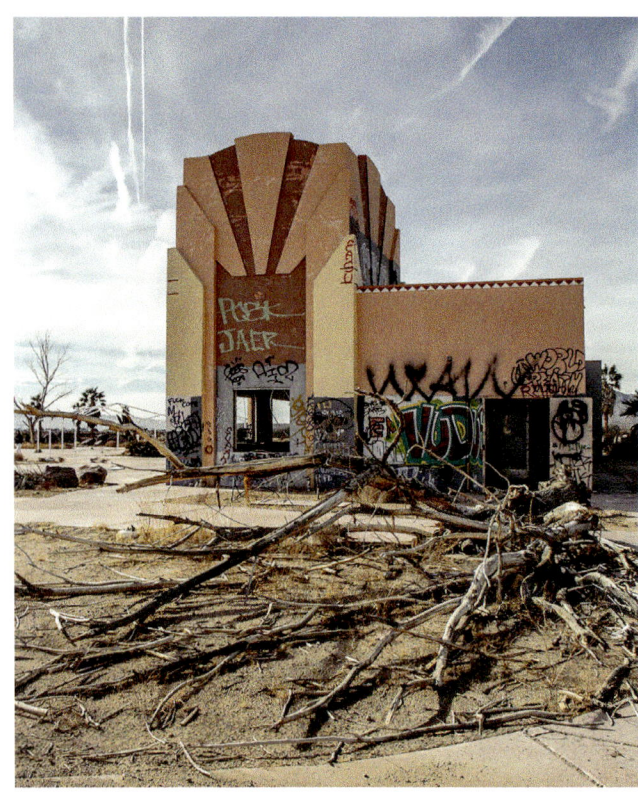

This building was constructed in the Rock-a-Hoola days of the park. It is created in a 1950s–1960s style to match the rebranding of the waterpark.

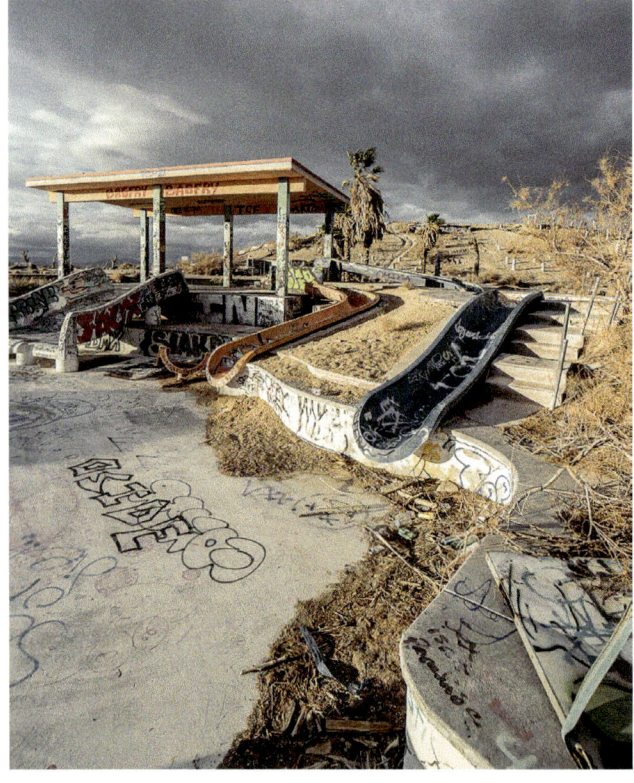

Some of the only remaining slides in the park. This area would have been catered to smaller children.

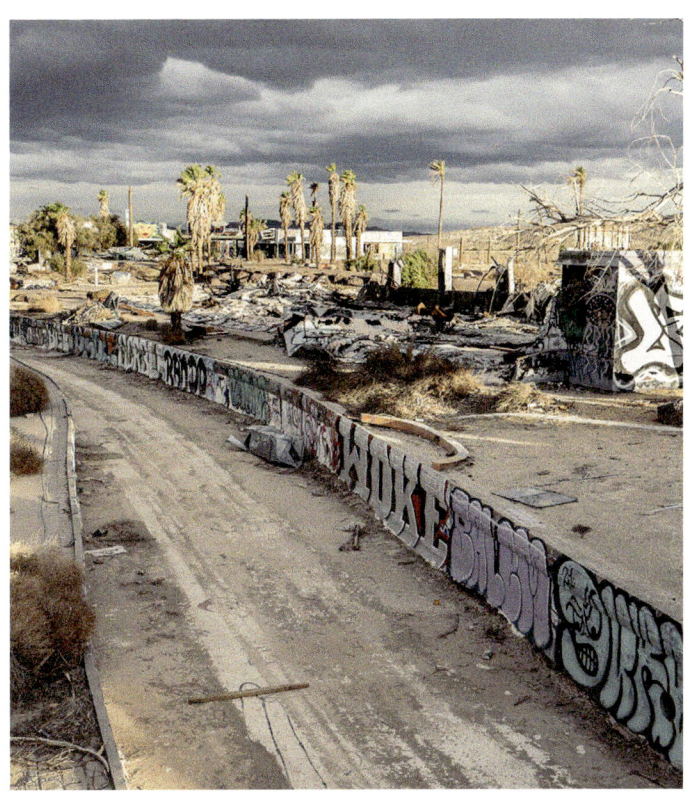

Looking down the lazy river.

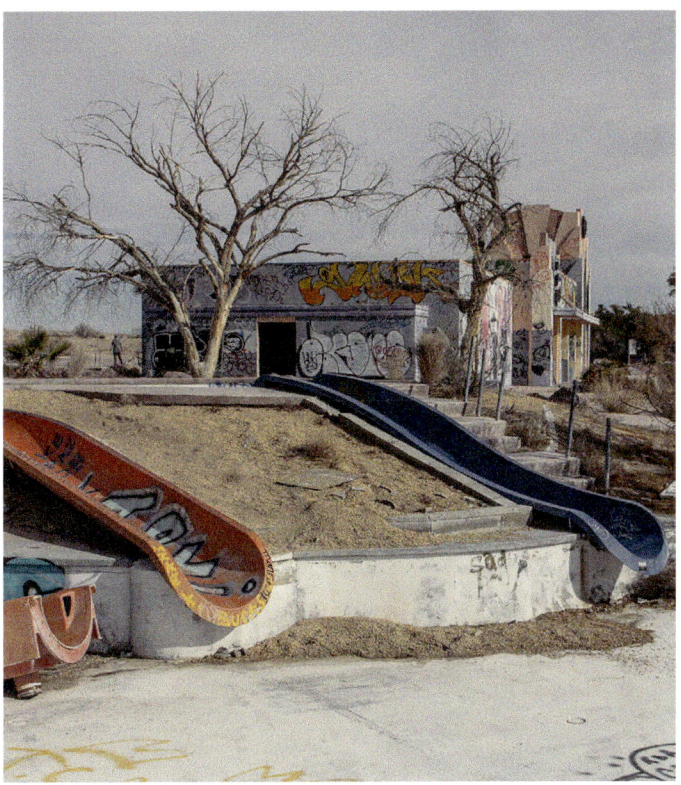

Children's slides.

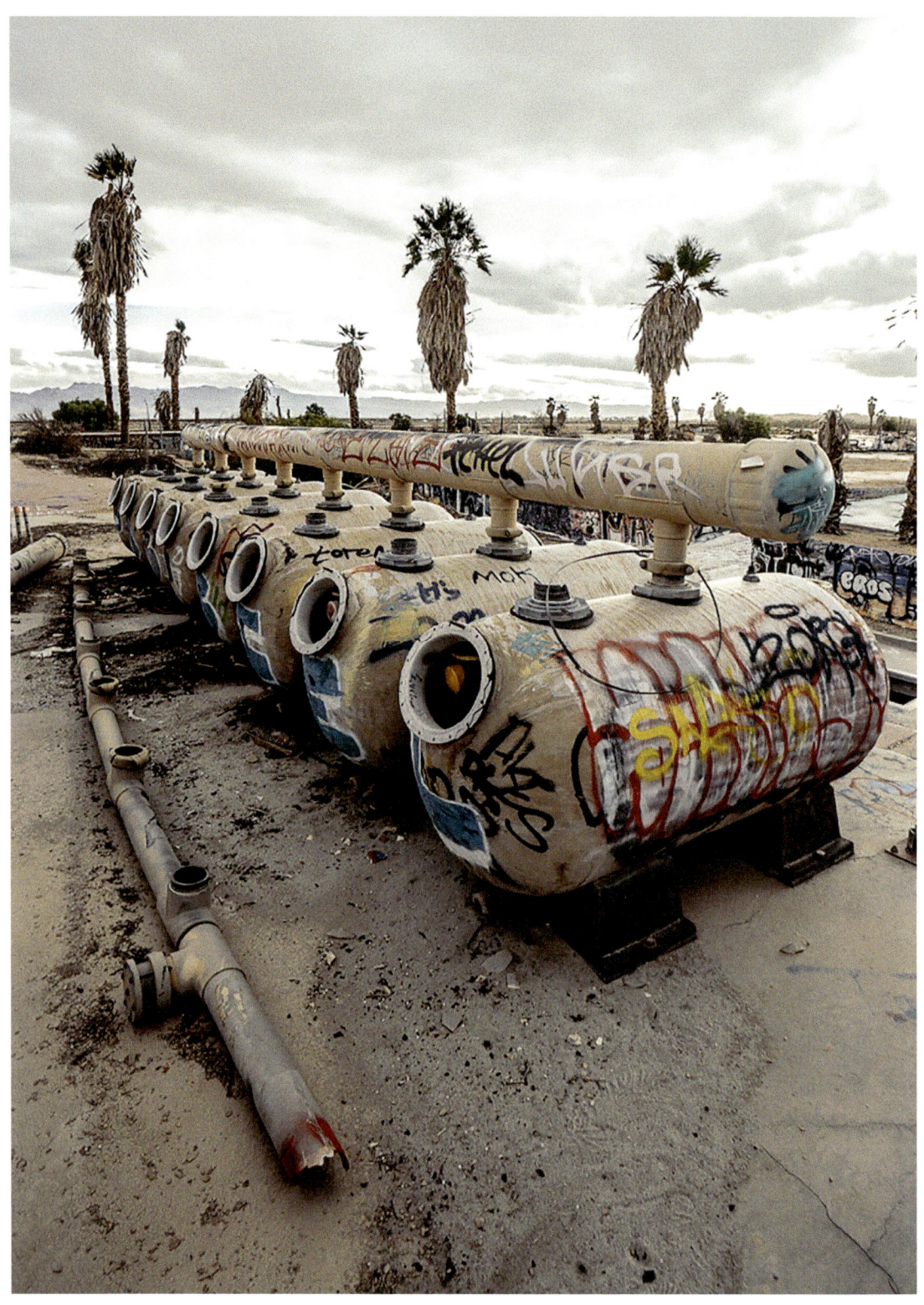

Part of the water pump and filtration system.

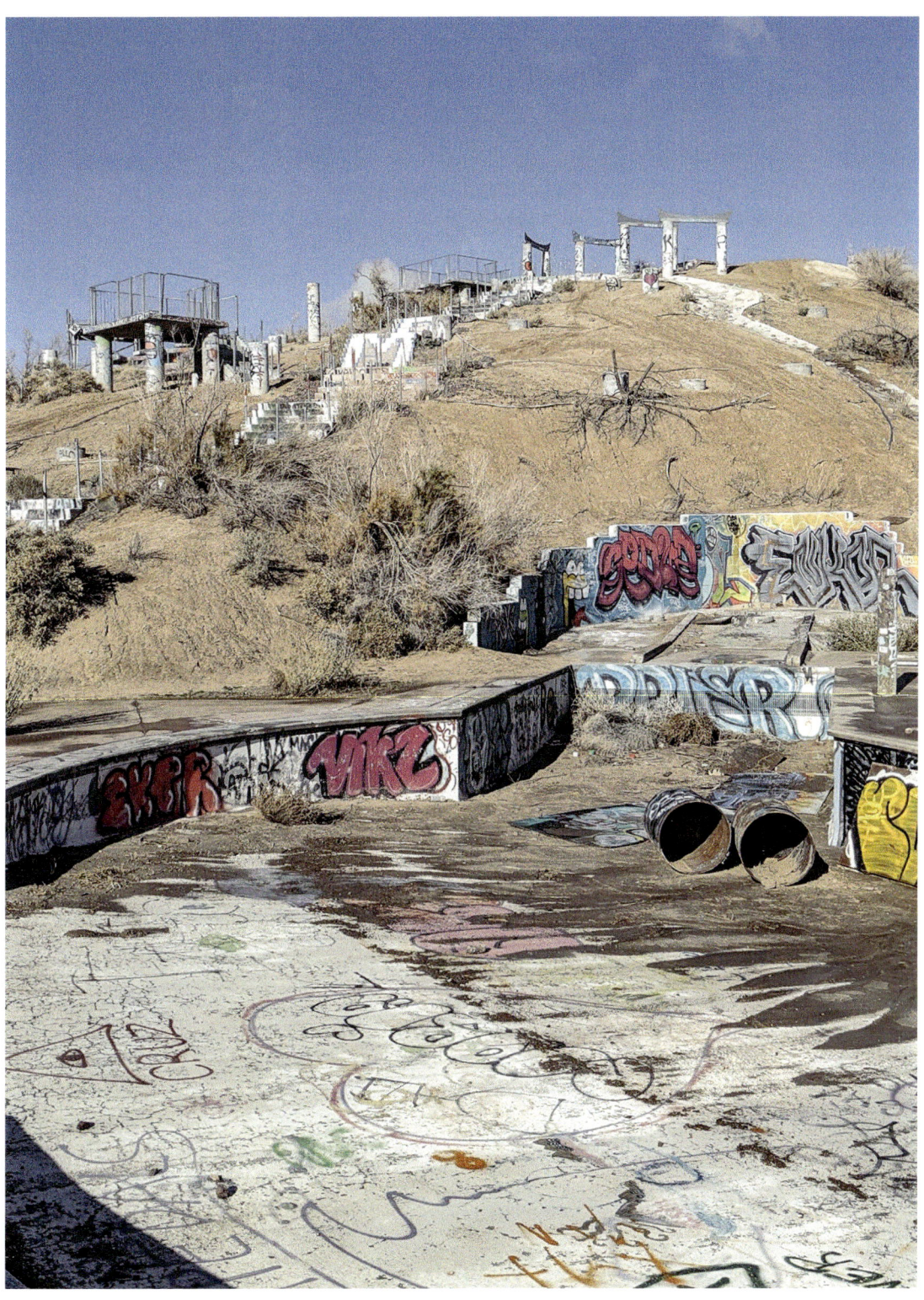

Looking up the hill towards the larger slides, this photo was taken a few years after the first photo of similar composition.

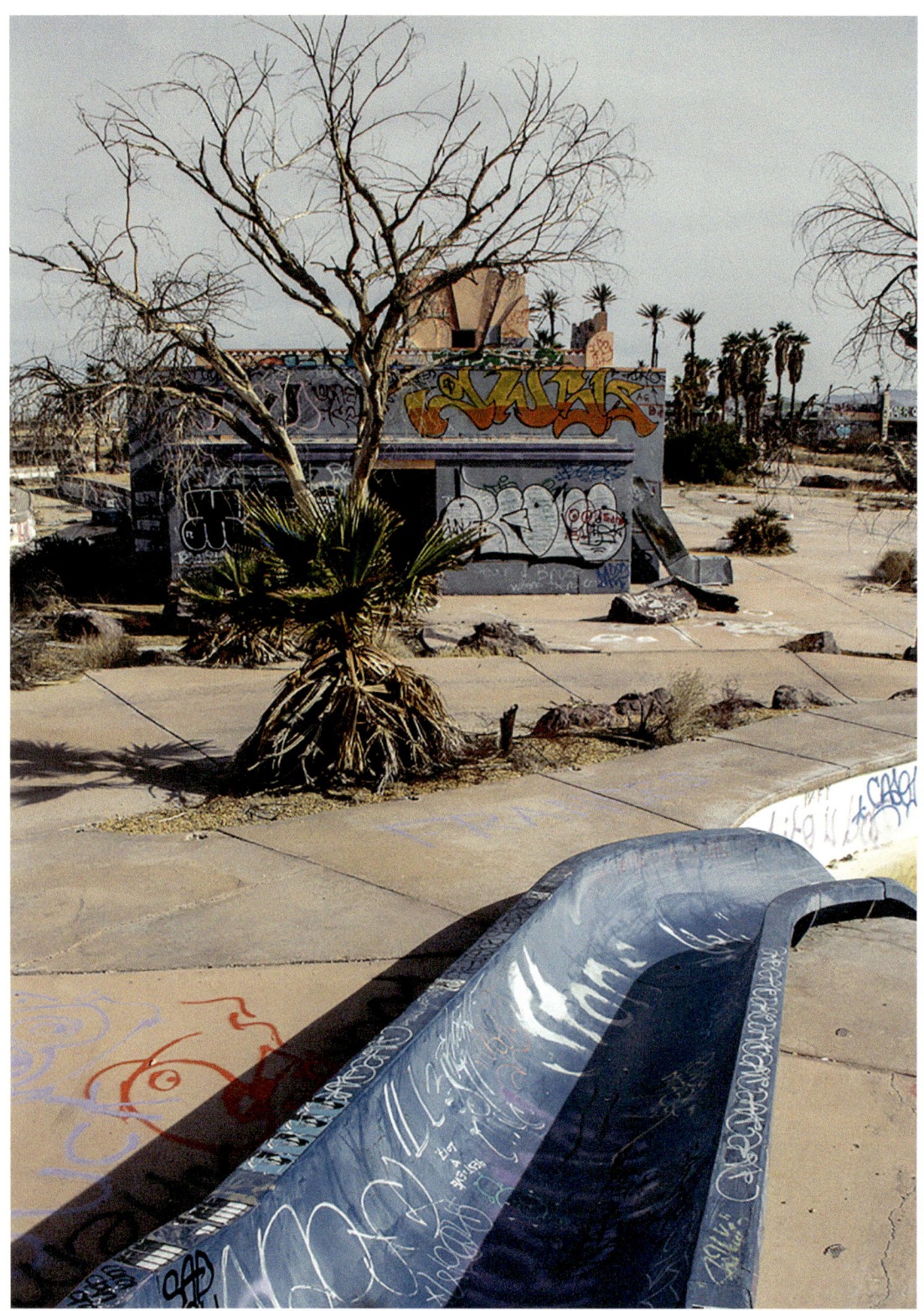

You can imagine families enjoying their summers here.

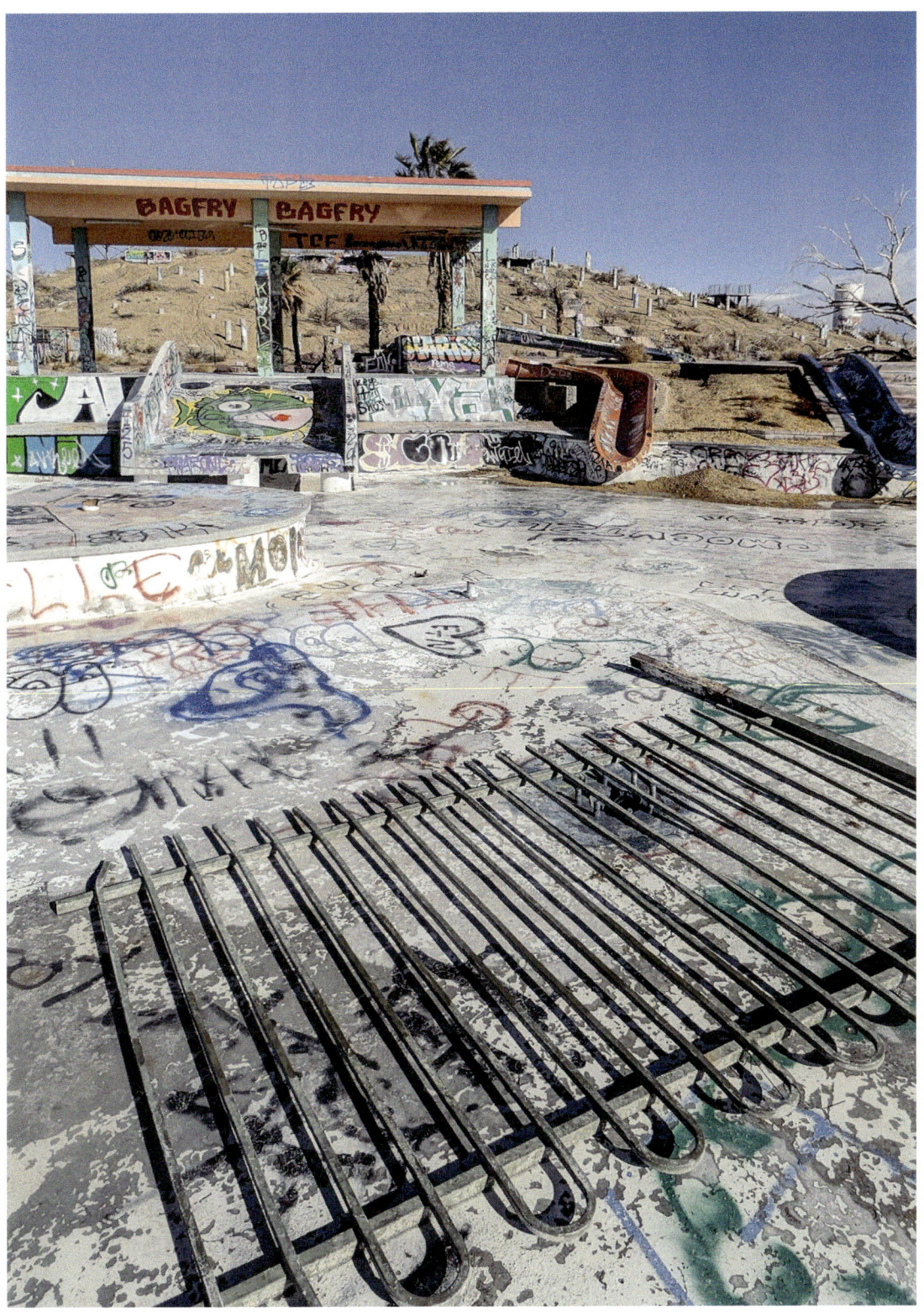

This area, as is the case with many abandoned places, has become a haven for graffiti artists.

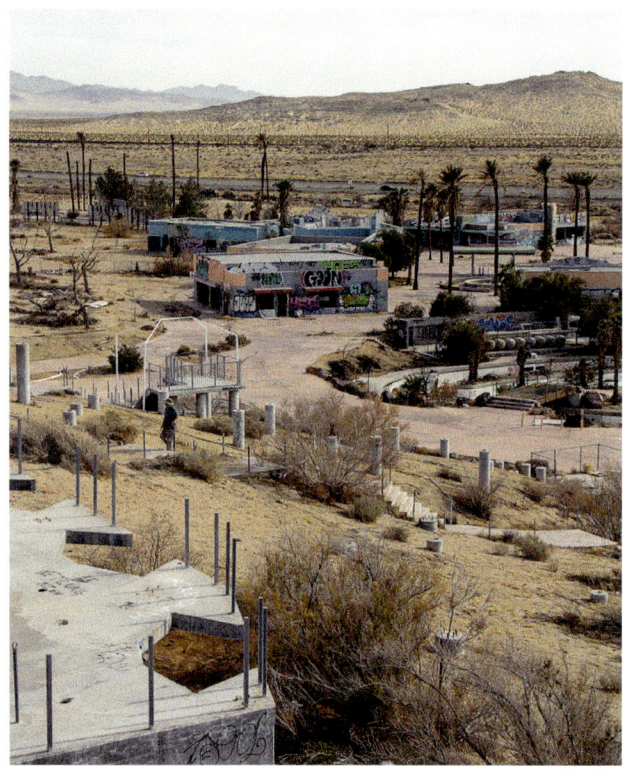

Looking down onto the waterpark grounds from the top of the big slide.

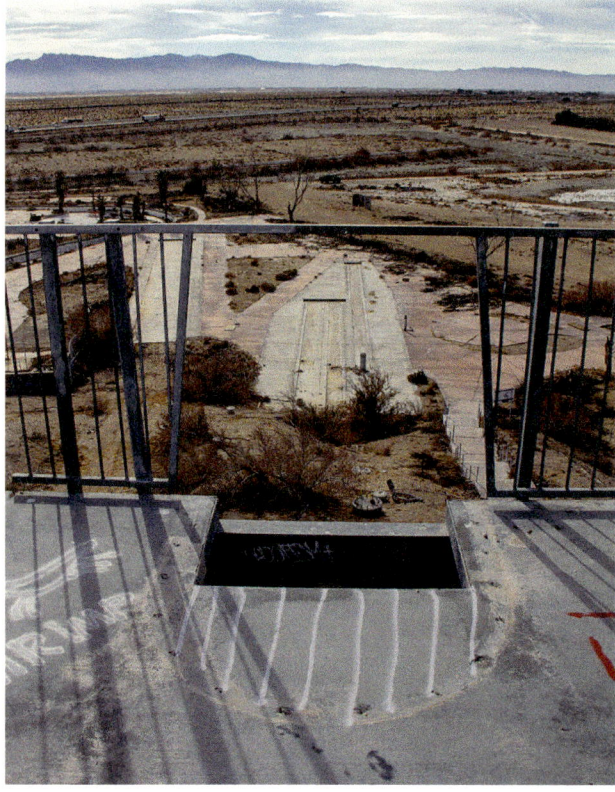

The path that riders would have used, when enjoying one of the largest slides on the property.

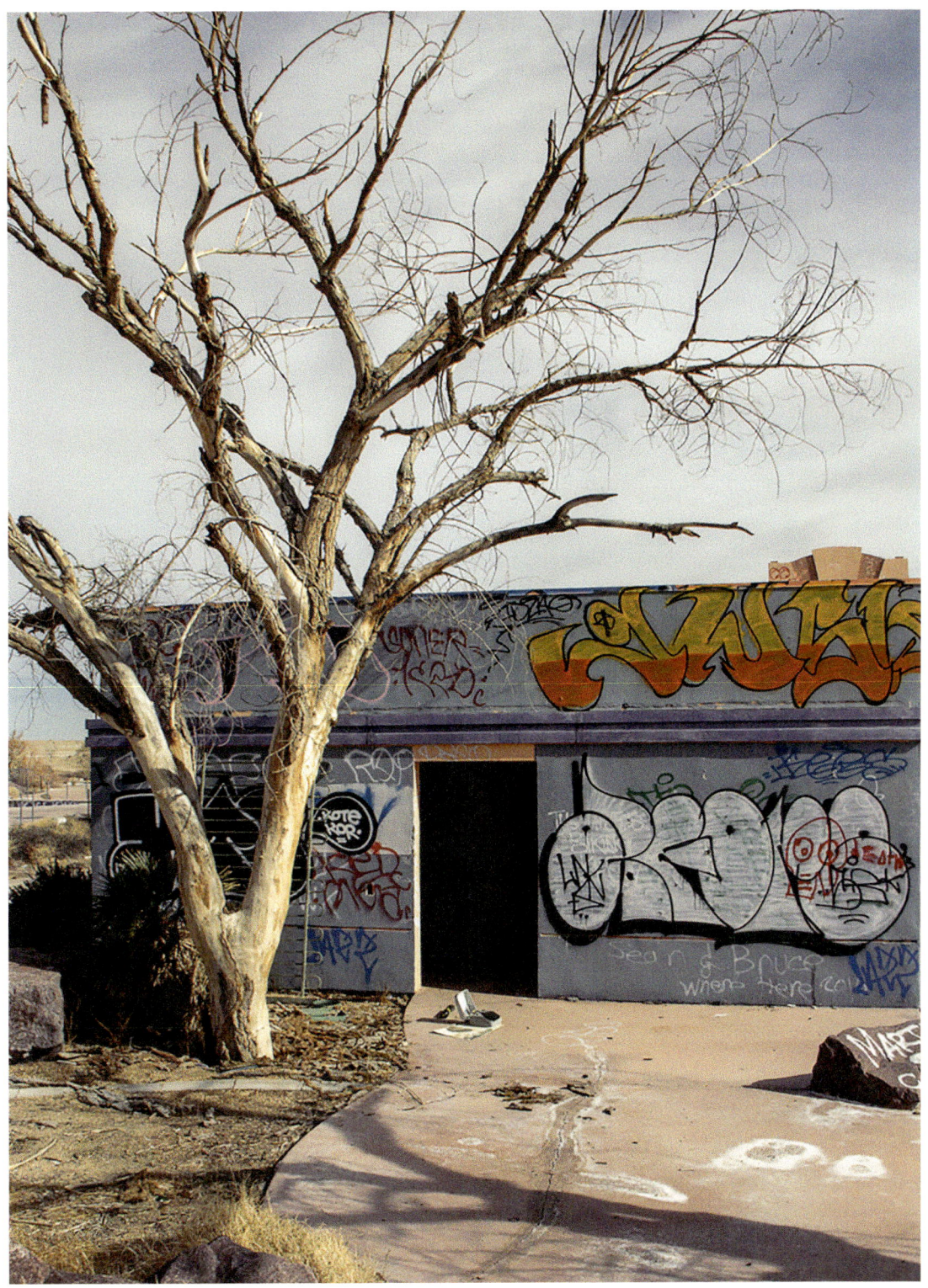

Once the waterpark closed, the owners stopped pumping water up from the Mojave Aquifer. It is surprising that these trees can survive with so little water.

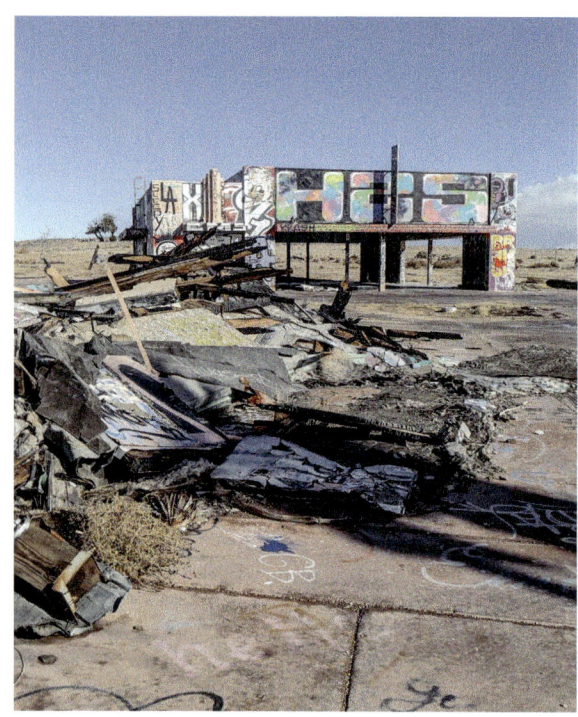

Left: One of the buildings that has recently fallen after a fire.

Below: Children's waterslides.

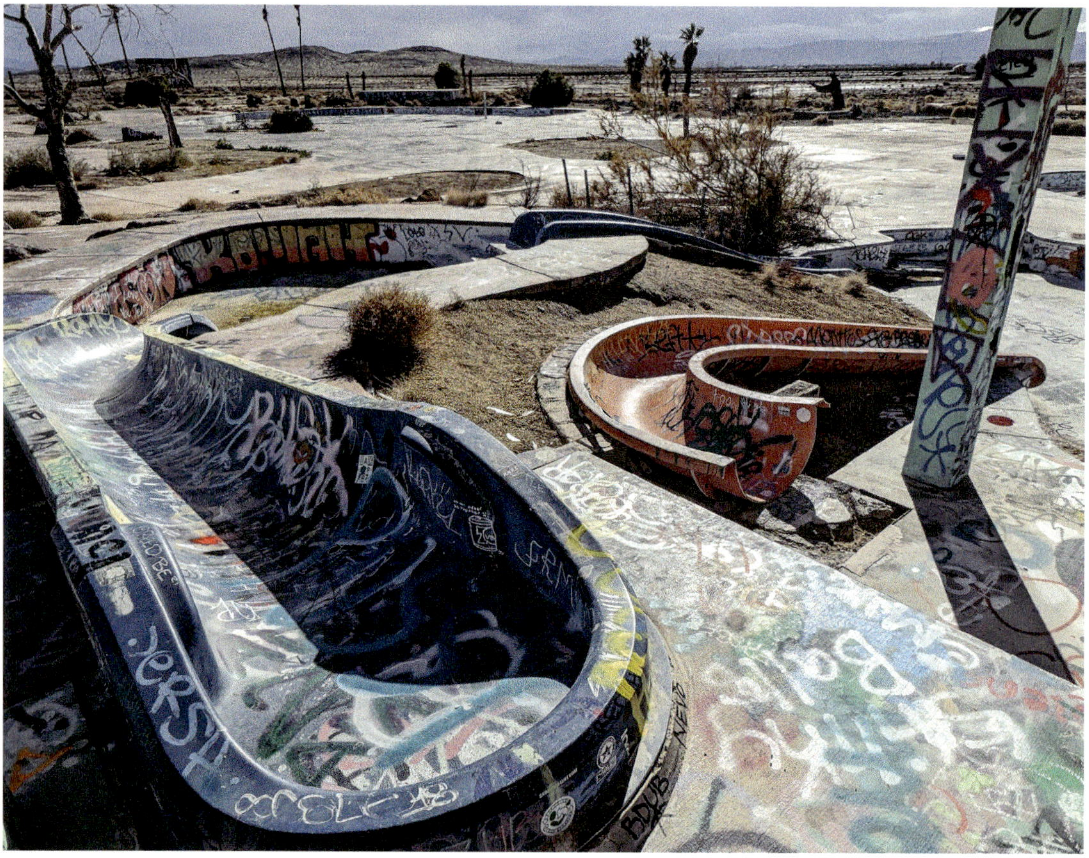

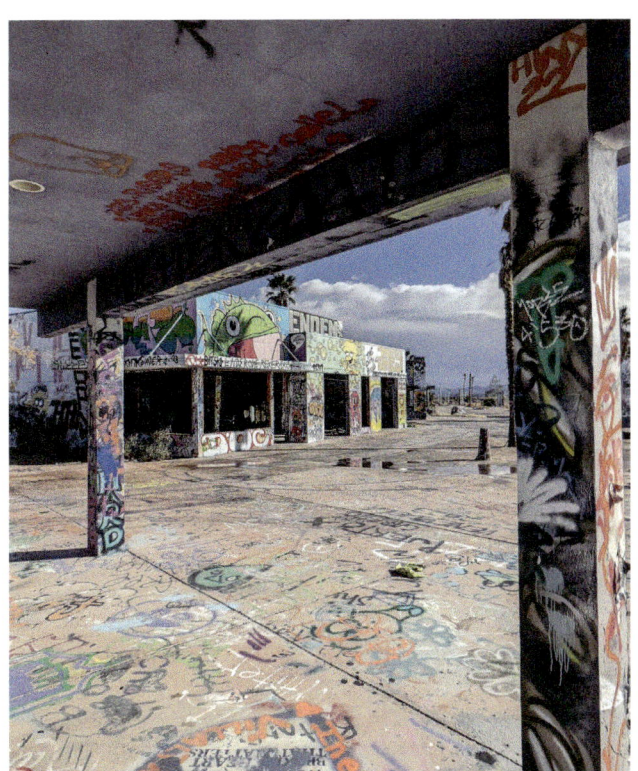

Right: Looking back at a building that would have housed games and souvenirs.

Below: Walking into the waterpark.

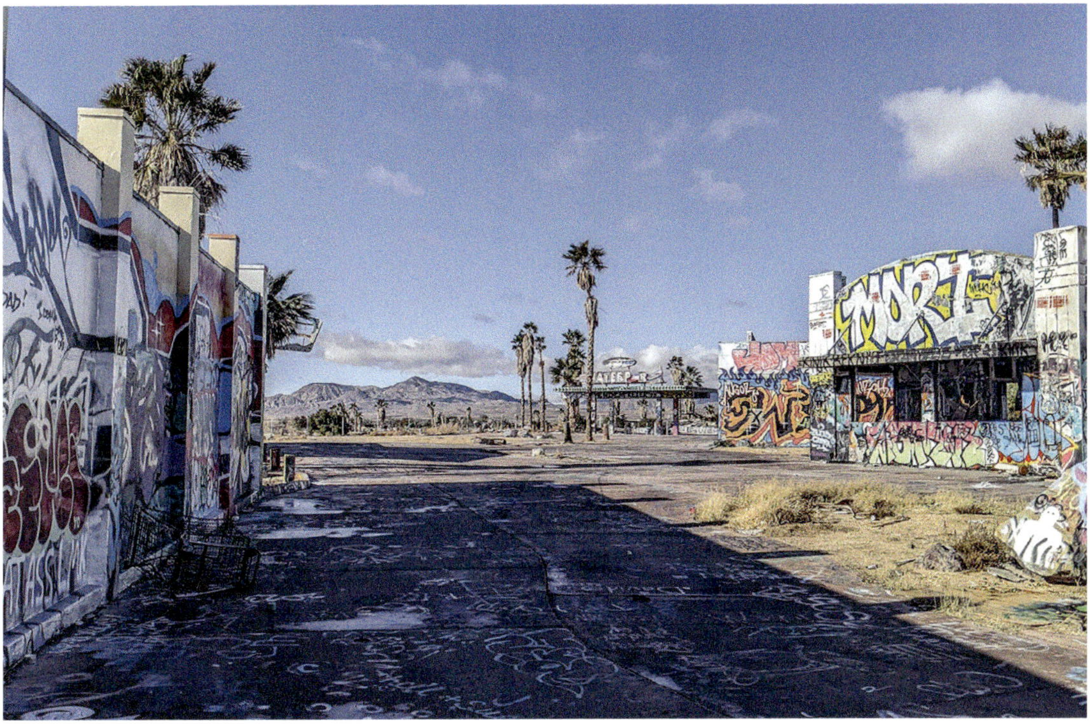

6

ARNIE'S ROYAL HAWAIIAN MOTEL: REMNANTS OF A BYGONE ERA

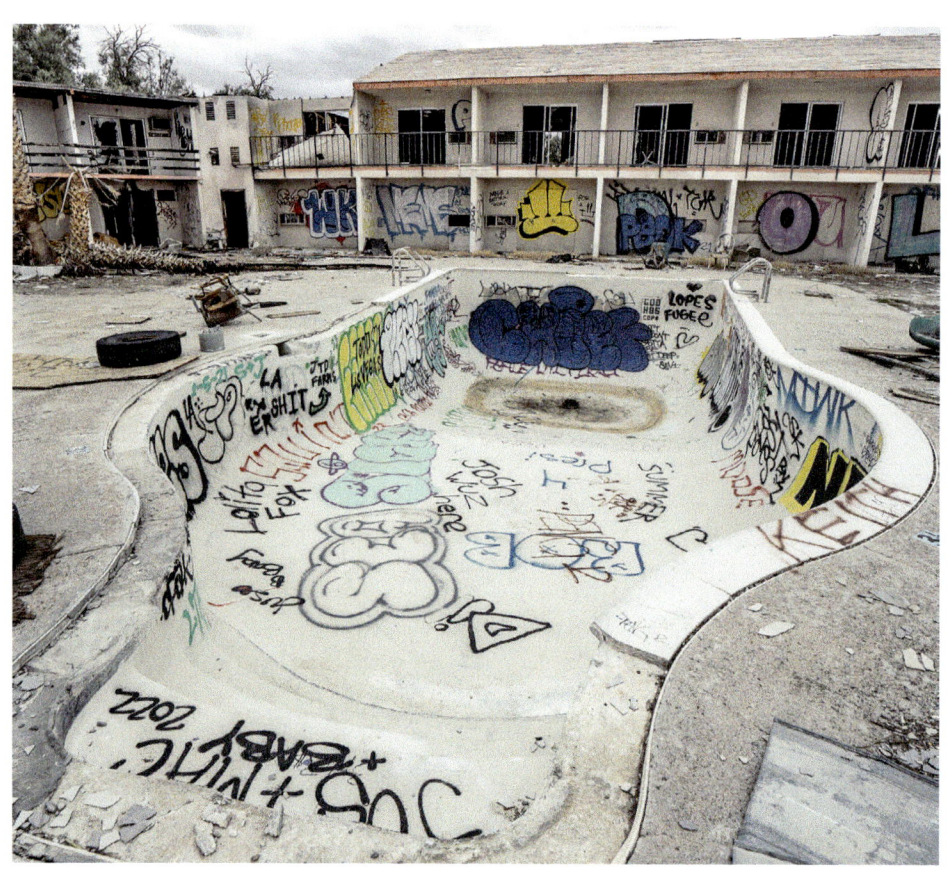

The pool at Arne's Royal Hawaiian Motel.

Abandoned motels along well-traveled routes are a common sight today. These neglected buildings, once bustling with activity, now silently decay by the roadside. With boarded-up windows and faded signs, they stand as relics of changing times and shifting priorities in travel.

Arnie's Royal Hawaiian Motel, born in 1957 amid the completion of the I-15 freeway linking Los Angeles to Las Vegas, stands as a stoic monument to these changing tides of travel preferences. Once a vibrant pit-stop along this bustling highway, Arnie's proudly showcased forty-three air-conditioned rooms, color televisions, two swimming pools, and a twenty-four-hour restaurant situated conveniently across the street.

As time passed, the trajectory of I-15 witnessed the ascension of competing regions. Arne's motel, which was once one of the only places of accommodation was losing its customers to newer, more alluring amenities. The once-thriving motel gradually succumbed to the shifting sands of preference. By 2008, the doors of the motel closed for the last time, leaving its halls to the mercy of abandonment.

The ravages of time and an unforgiving fire have left their indelible mark on Arnie's. The main structure, now a skeletal framework, bears the scars of a roof that has collapsed in multiple places. The air is thick with a palpable sense of desolation, and only faint echoes of transient habitation remain, scattered traces left behind by those who sought refuge within its dilapidated embrace.

As the present-day traffic rushes past on the nearby interstate, Arnie's Royal Hawaiian Motel stands as a reminder of a bygone era. Each weathered board and peeling paint layer tell a story of a time when this place was a sanctuary for weary travelers. Amid the quiet decay, the motel becomes a visual metaphor for the transience of human constructs in the face of progress.

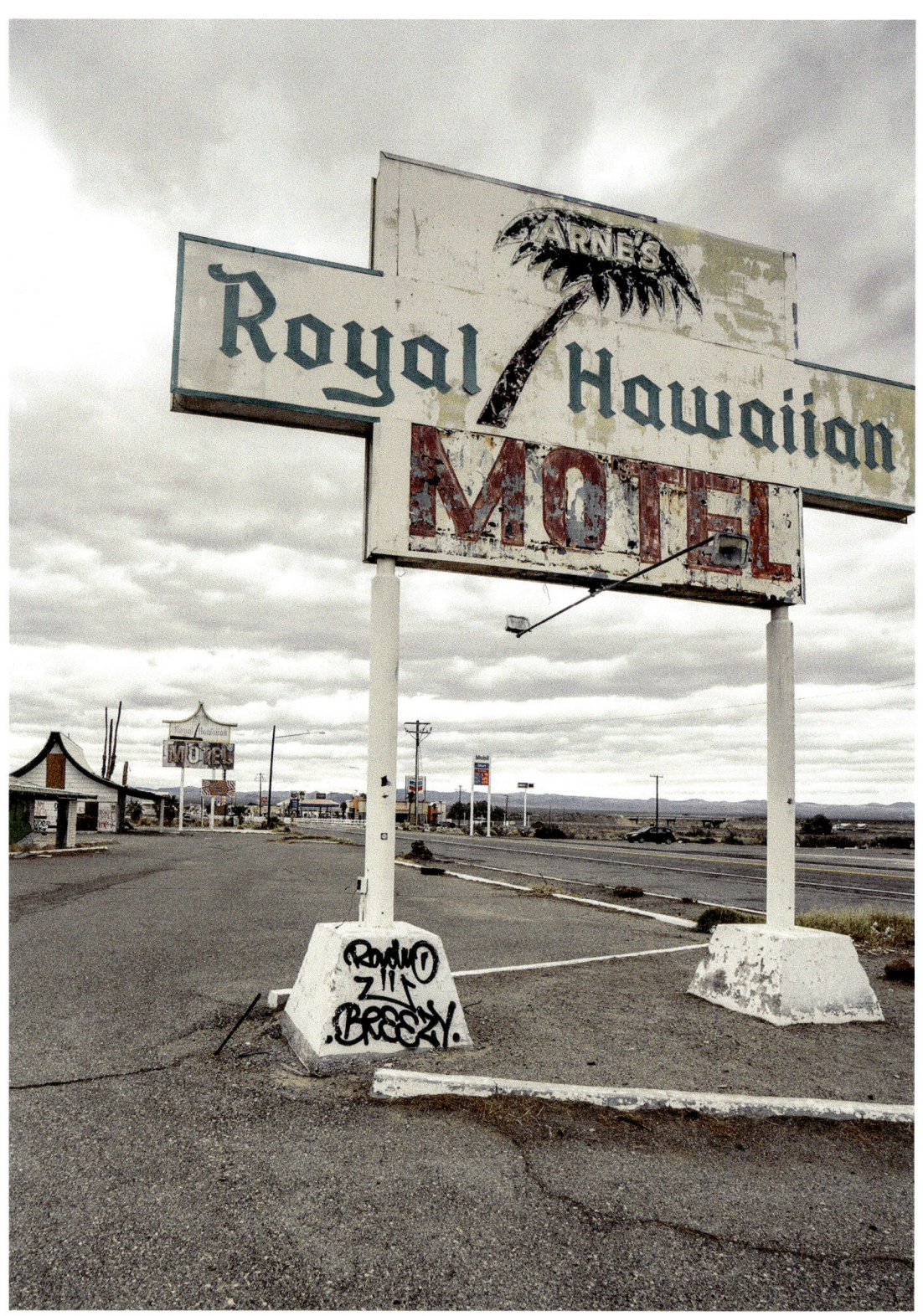

This sign would have greeted weary travelers as they pulled into the motel.

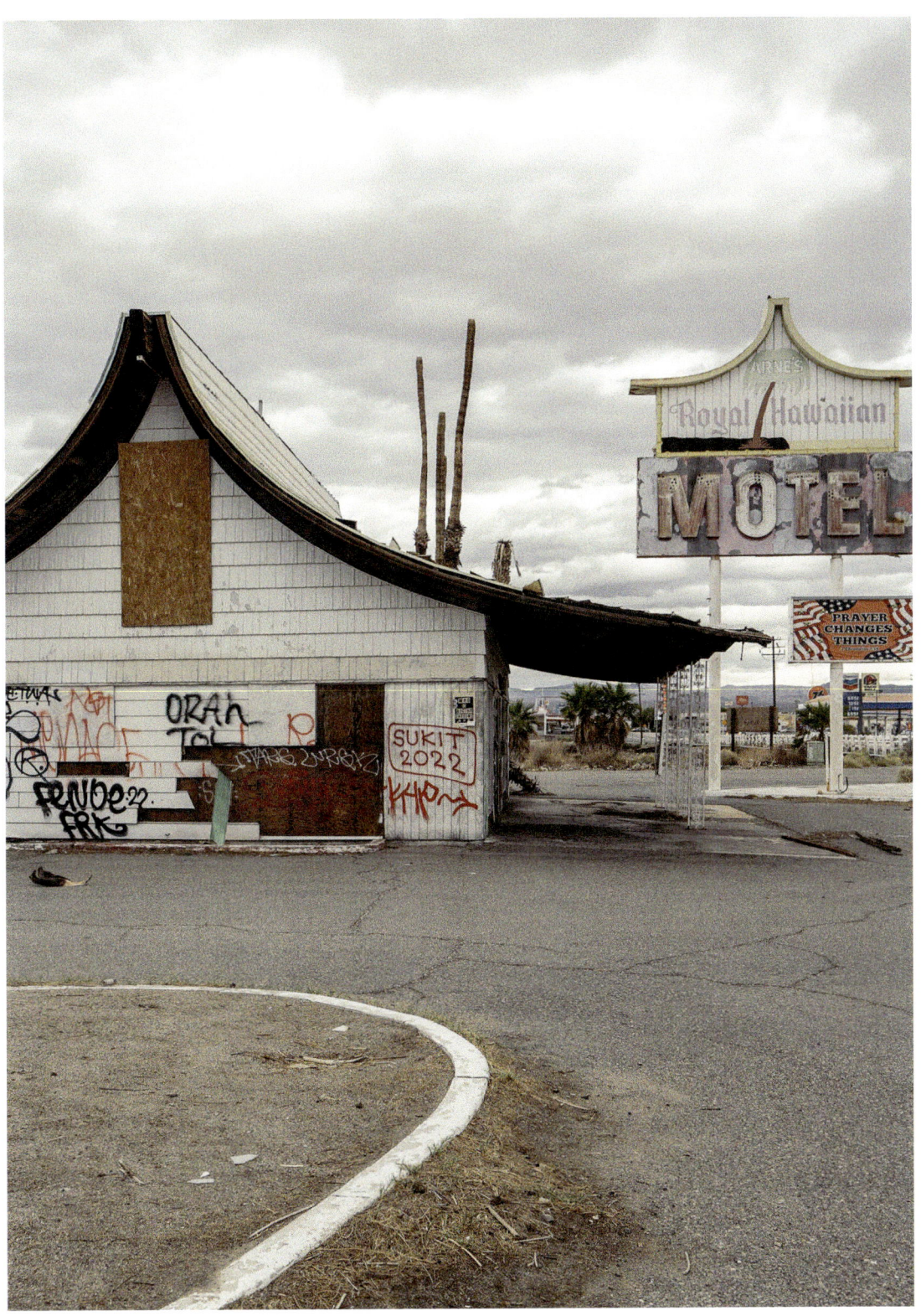

The lobby of Arne's Royal Hawaiian Motel.

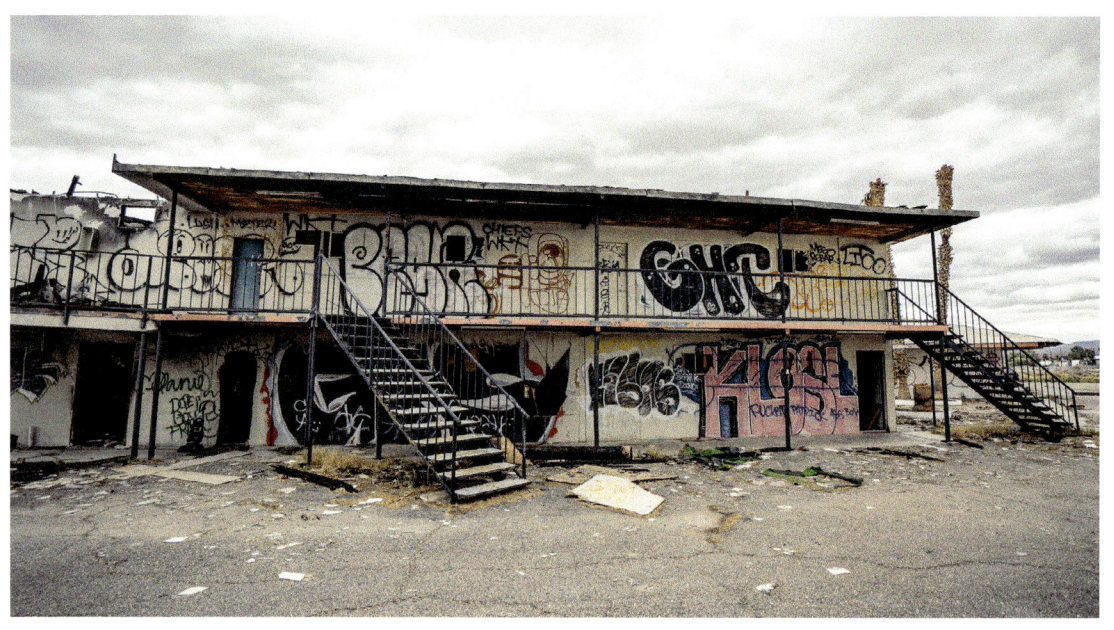

Stairs to the second floor of one of the remaining buildings.

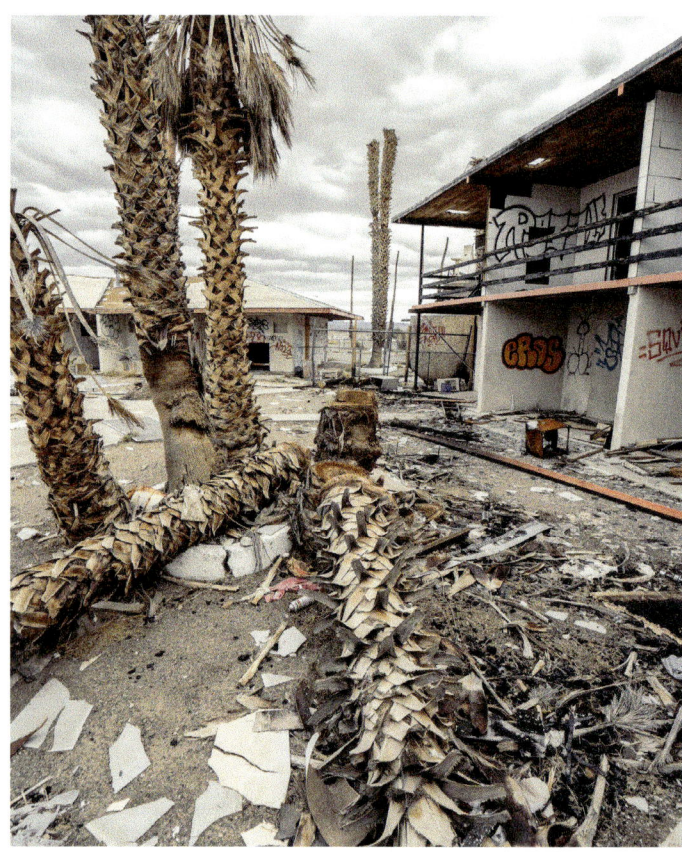

At one point, there would have been palm trees all over the property, keeping up with the Hawaiian theme of the motel. Today, many of these trees have fallen.

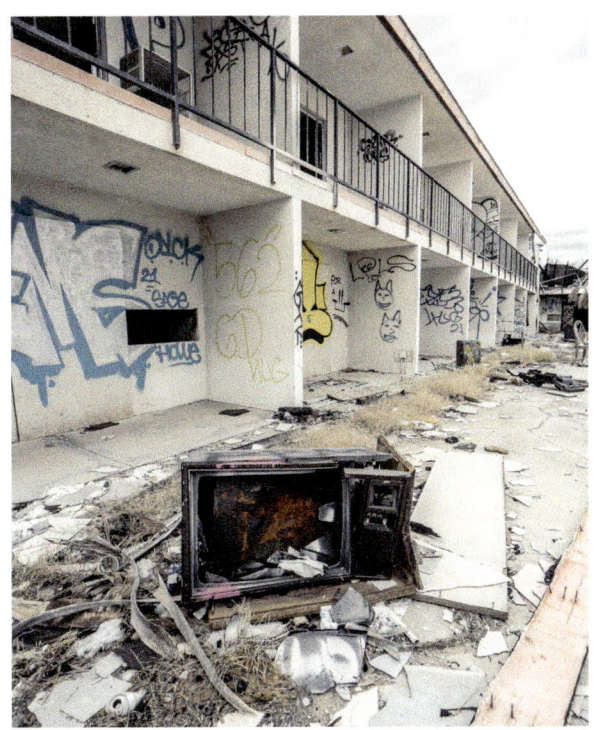

A television from one of the rooms now sits on the ground by the pool.

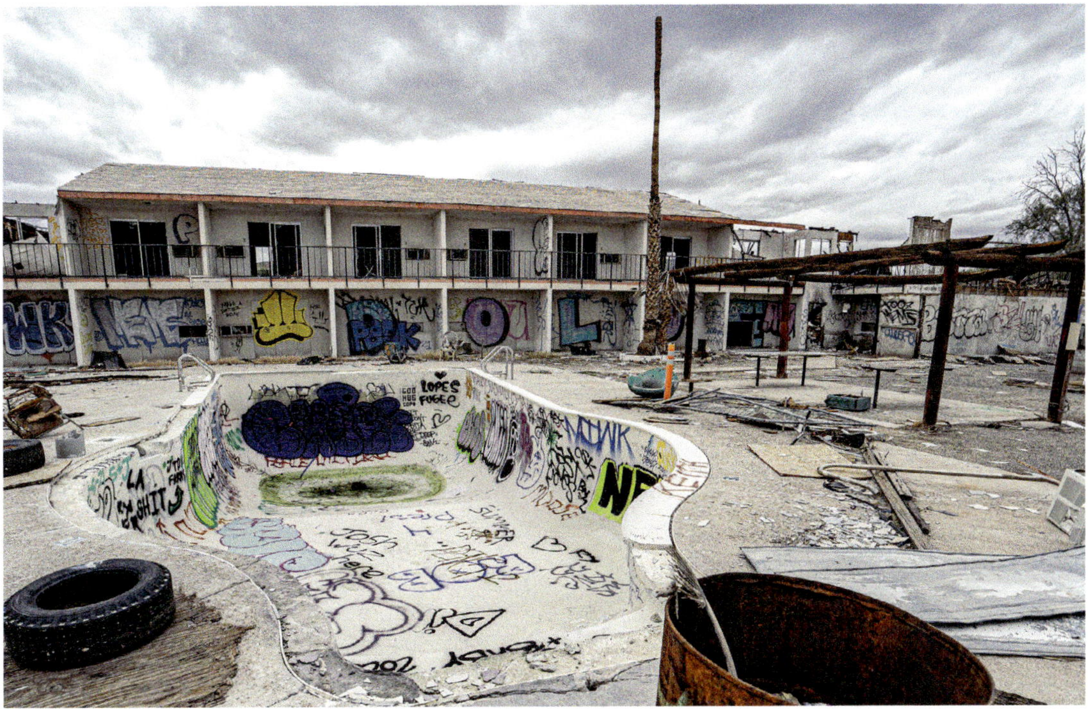

Looking over the main courtyard and pool area, there was a pergola and barbeque area next to the pool.

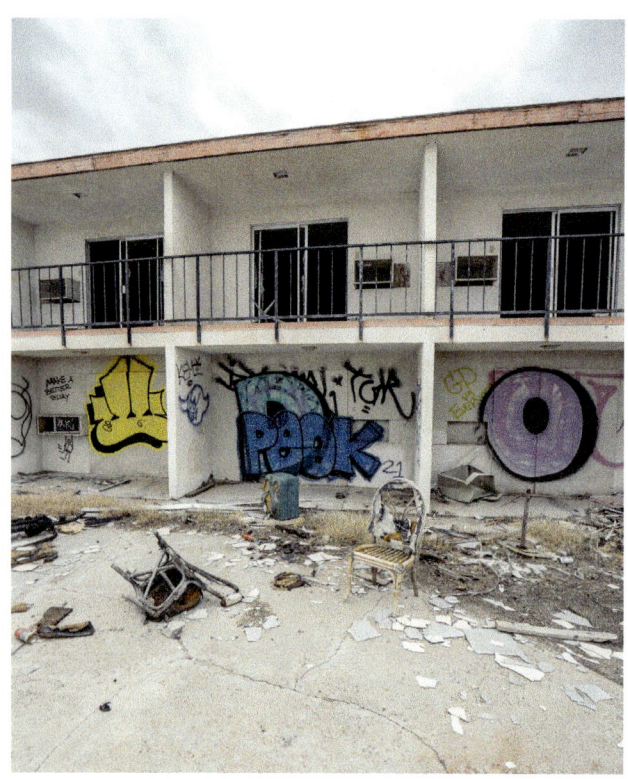

Boarded-up hotel rooms.

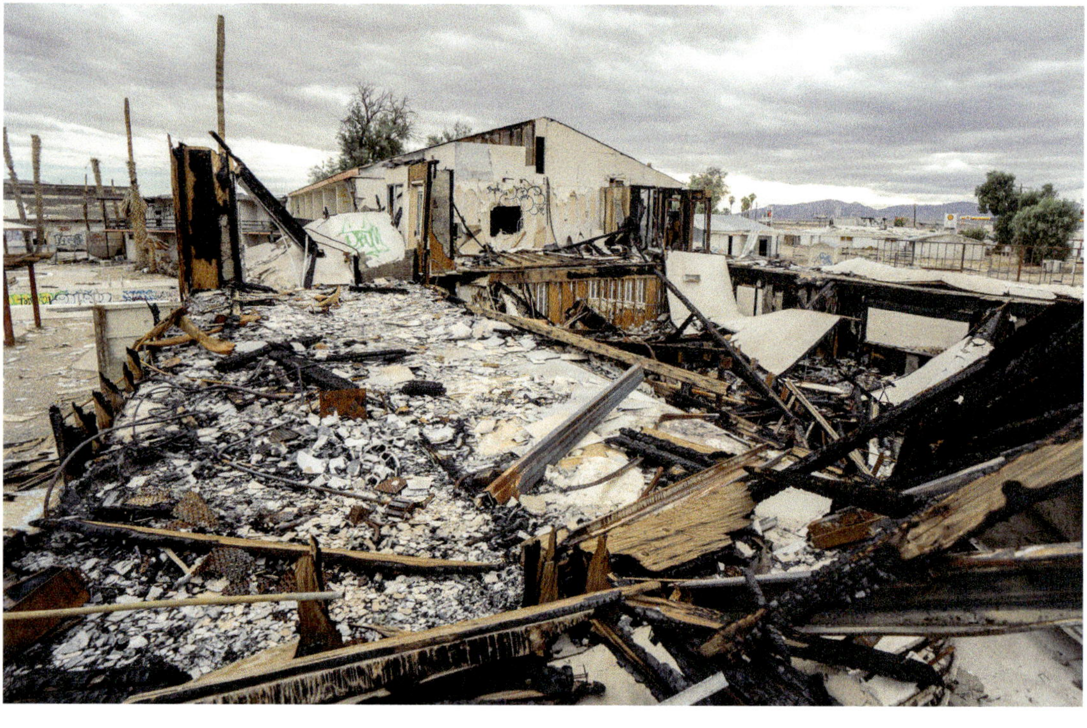

A fire has destroyed the back section of the motel, causing a collapse.

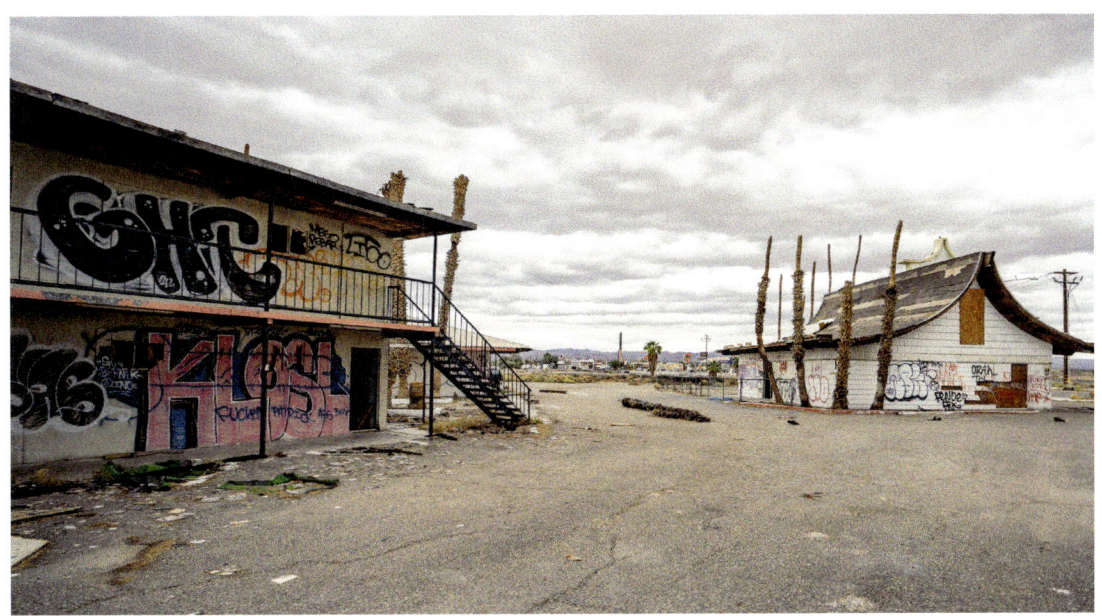

Parking lot and check-in.

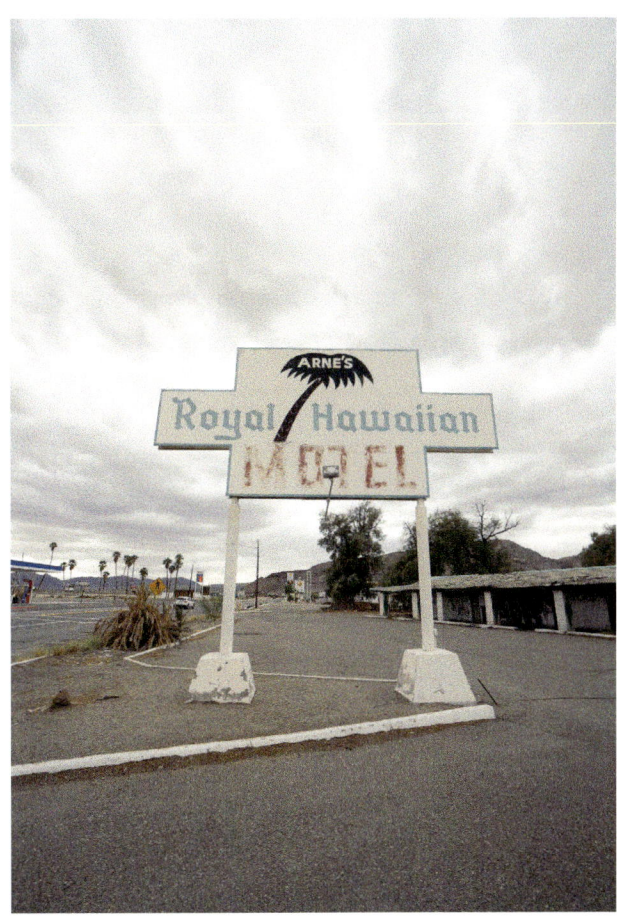

Motel sign.

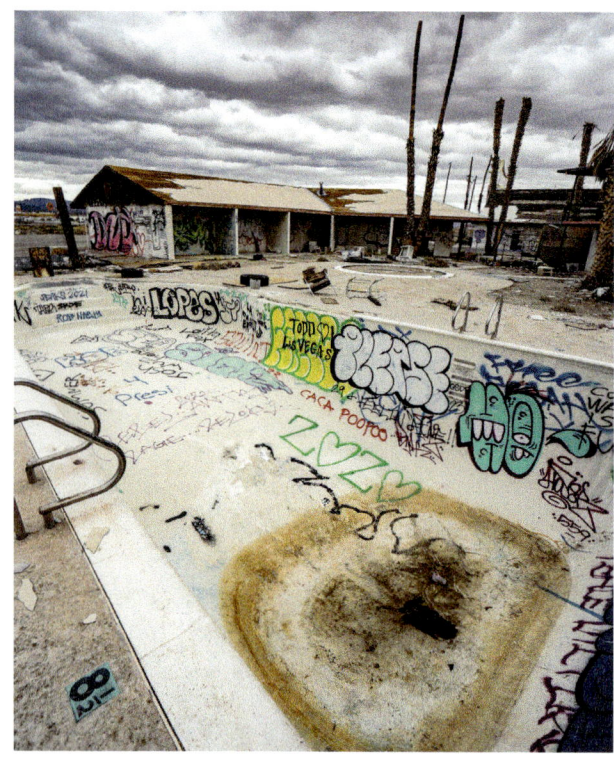

The pool and patio.

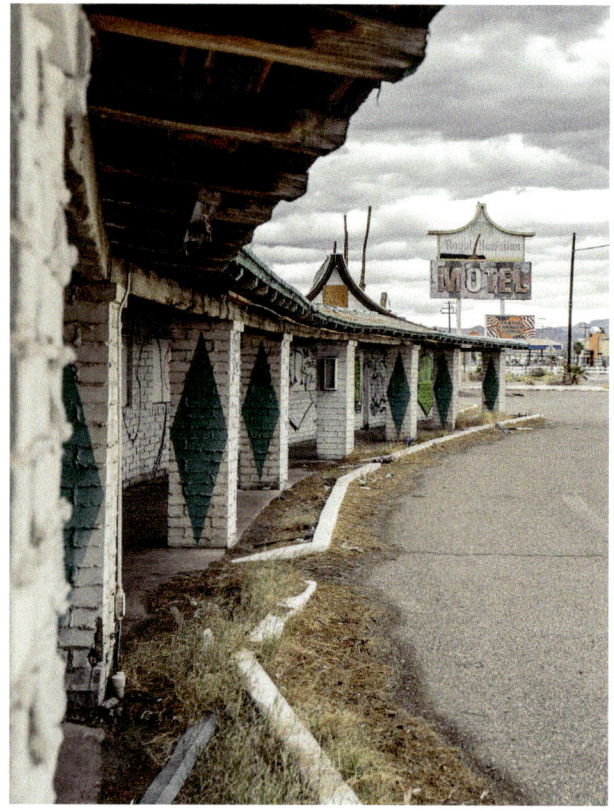

This section of rooms was the first built at the motel, before the other additions were constructed. These rooms lined the road.

7

BALLARAT GHOST TOWN: A MINING TOWN WITH A DARK HISTORY

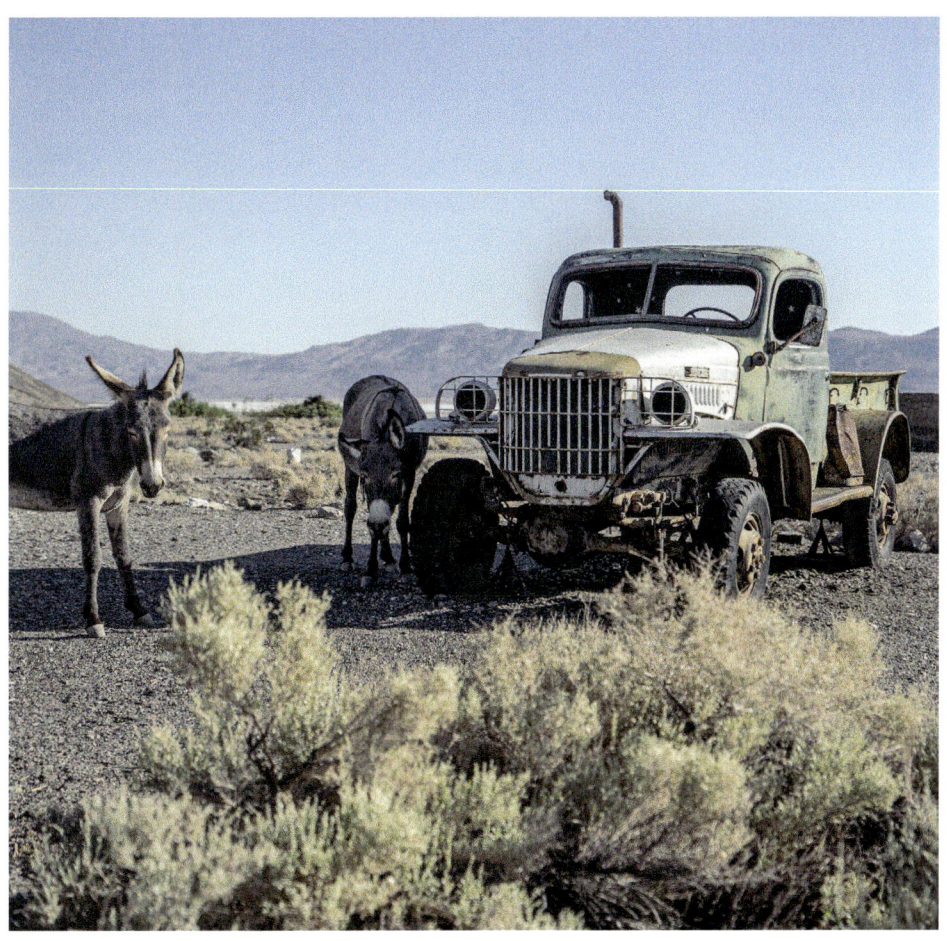

The "Manson Family Truck" and wild burros.

In the heart of the Panamint Mountain Range, stands the ghostly remnant of Ballarat. Established in 1897, this once-thriving town emerged from the dust to supply the mining operations that echoed through the rugged peaks nearby. At its peak, Ballarat flourished with a bustling population that exceeded 400, fostering a community that boasted seven saloons, three hotels, a jail, a morgue, and a school.

The prosperity of Ballarat, however, was as ephemeral as the desert winds that swept through its streets. Less than two decades after its founding, the resounding closure of most mines in the Panamint Mountain Range cast a pall over the town's vibrant spirit. Yet, amid the abandonment, a few resilient prospectors lingered, determined to live in the shadow of Ballarat's faded glory.

One of these such residents was Charles Ferge, also known as Seldom Seen Slim. Slim held the unique distinction of being the lone inhabitant of Ballarat from around 1918 until his passing in 1968. Slim, renowned for his eccentric lifestyle, asserted that he had not taken a proper bath in two decades, as water was so scarce in the region. He lived in the only remaining adobe building until that too succumbed to decay, at which point Slim resorted to living in a Volkswagen.

As the town settled into a quiet slumber, Ballarat found itself touched by a darker chapter in its history during the 1960s. The infamous Charles Manson and his followers, known as the Manson Family, set up residence on a ranch not far from Ballarat. Living a mere whisper away from the town, they frequently visited Ballerat to procure supplies. Their unsettling presence left an indelible mark in the form of an infamous signature—a group of stars—etched on the inside of a truck parked in the quiet streets of Ballarat. To this day, this eerie relic remains as a testament to the unforeseen encounters that can shape the destiny of a quiet ghost town.

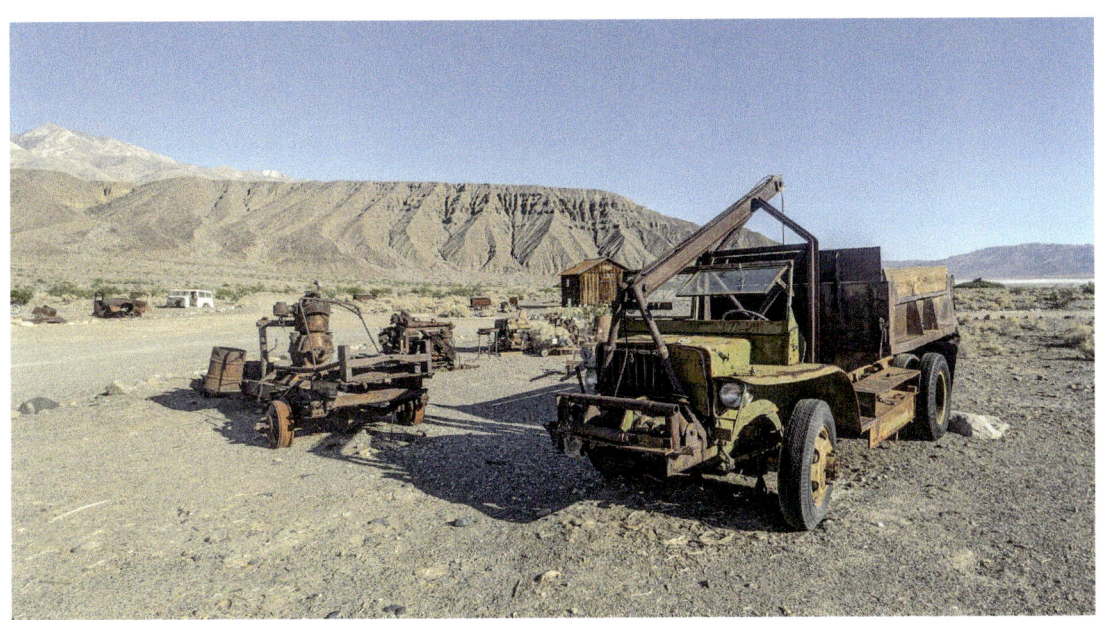

The caretakers have collected several vehicles left behind from the nearby mining operations of the Panamint mountain range. They have displayed them in town.

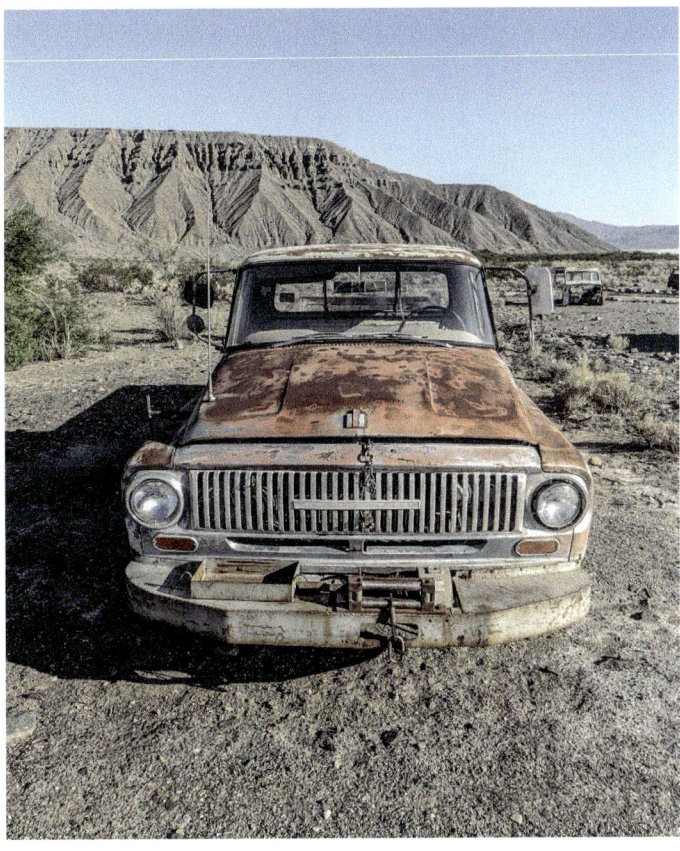

International truck.

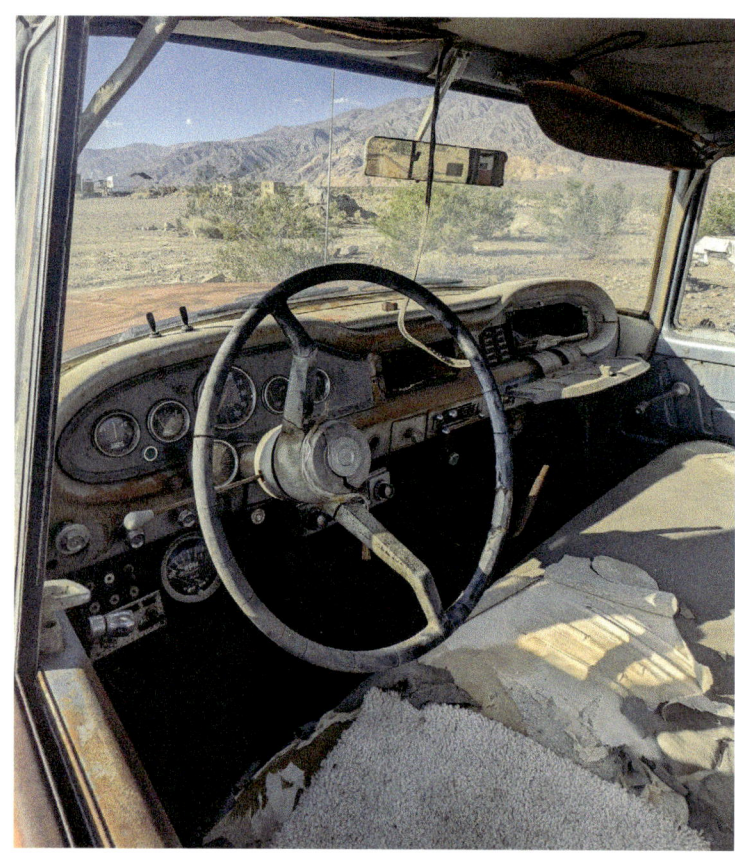

Inside the International.

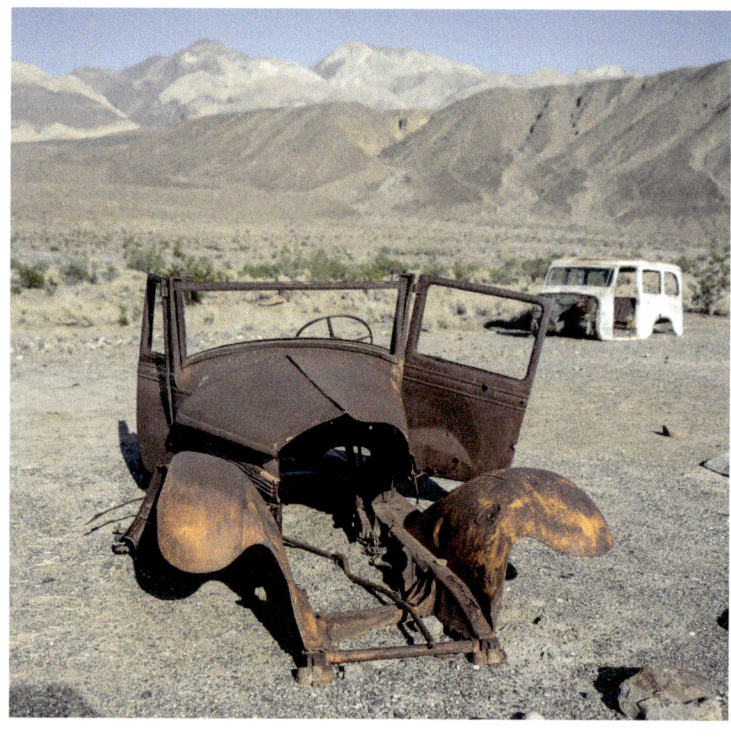

The bodies of cars,
separated from their frames.

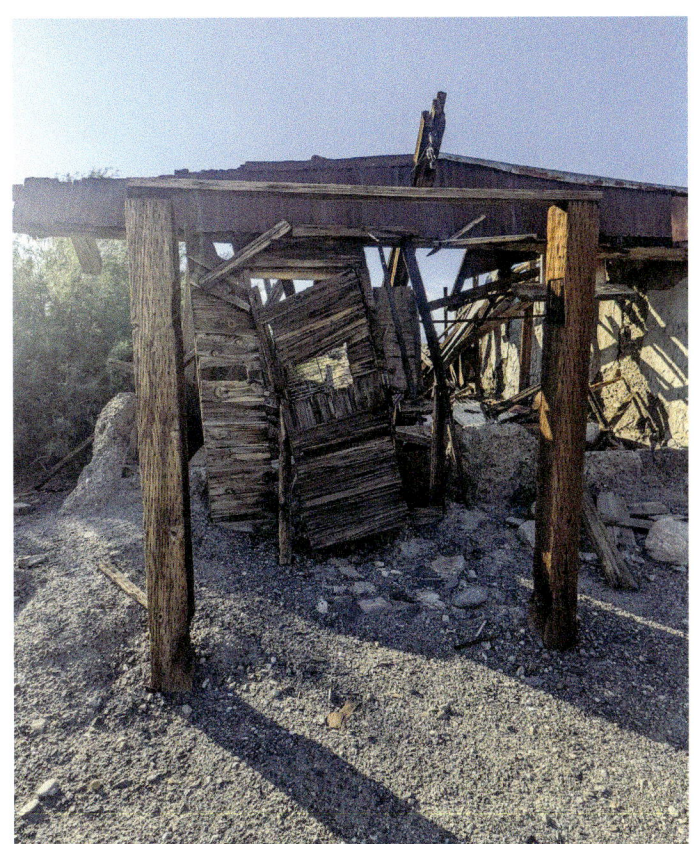

One of the remaining structures, most likely a family home at one point. You can see how weathered the wood has become from the harsh desert environment.

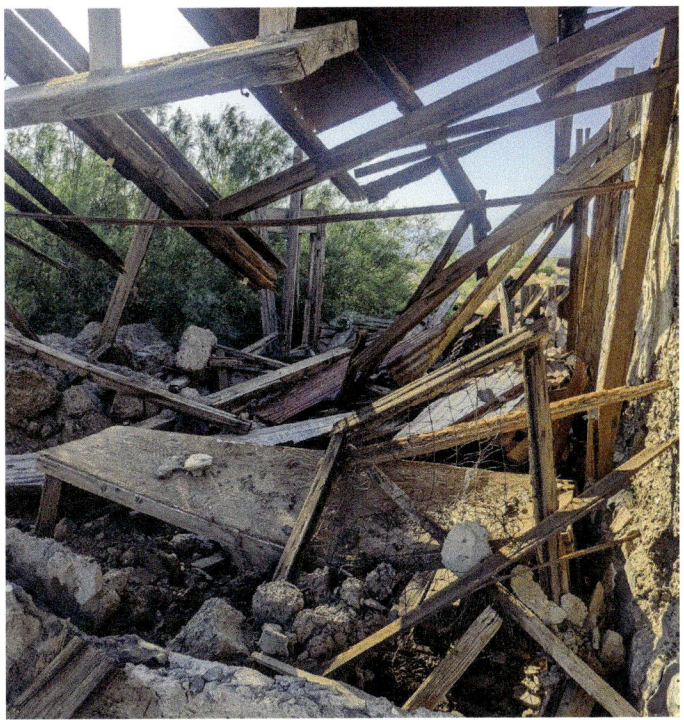

Collapsed roof of a miner's home.

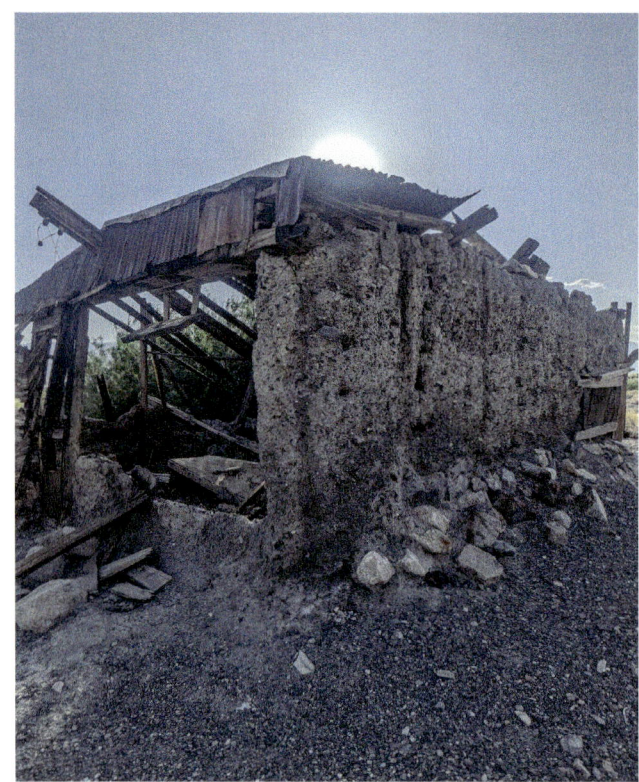

Adobe-style dwellings were popular in this area, as they were easy to build with the materials at hand.

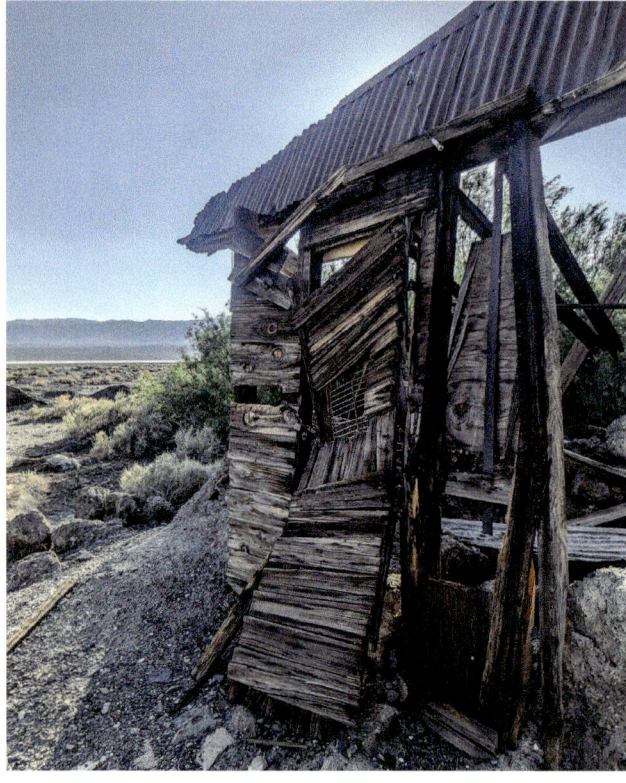

The front door.

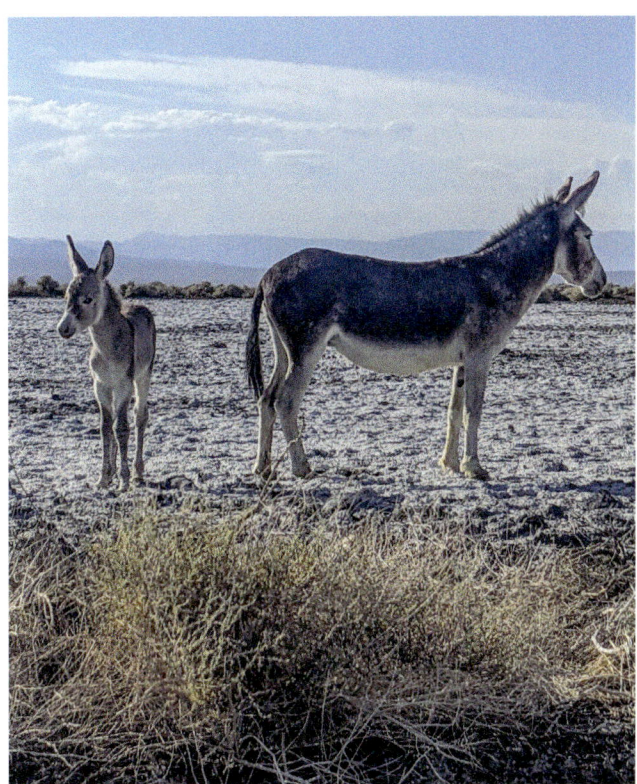

Wild burros, left behind from mining operations, have reproduced and now wander the streets of the ghost town.

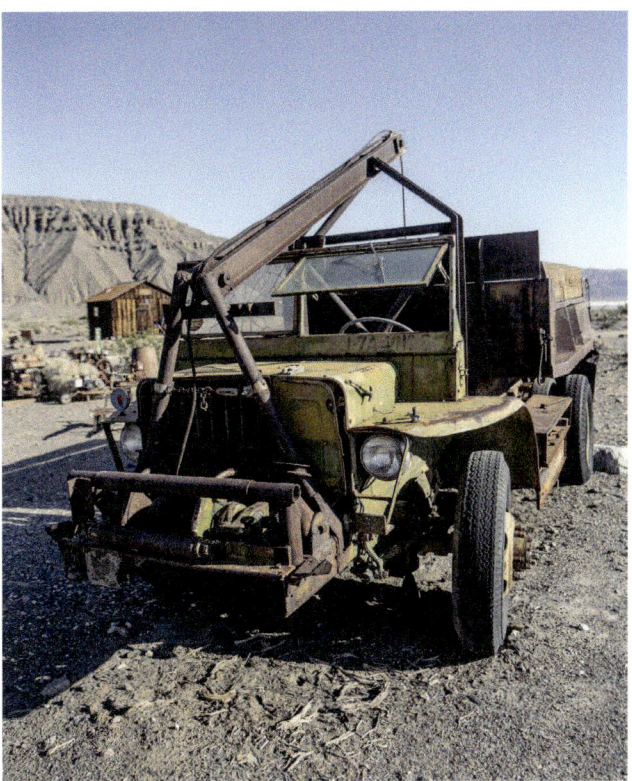

Old dump truck with a winch.

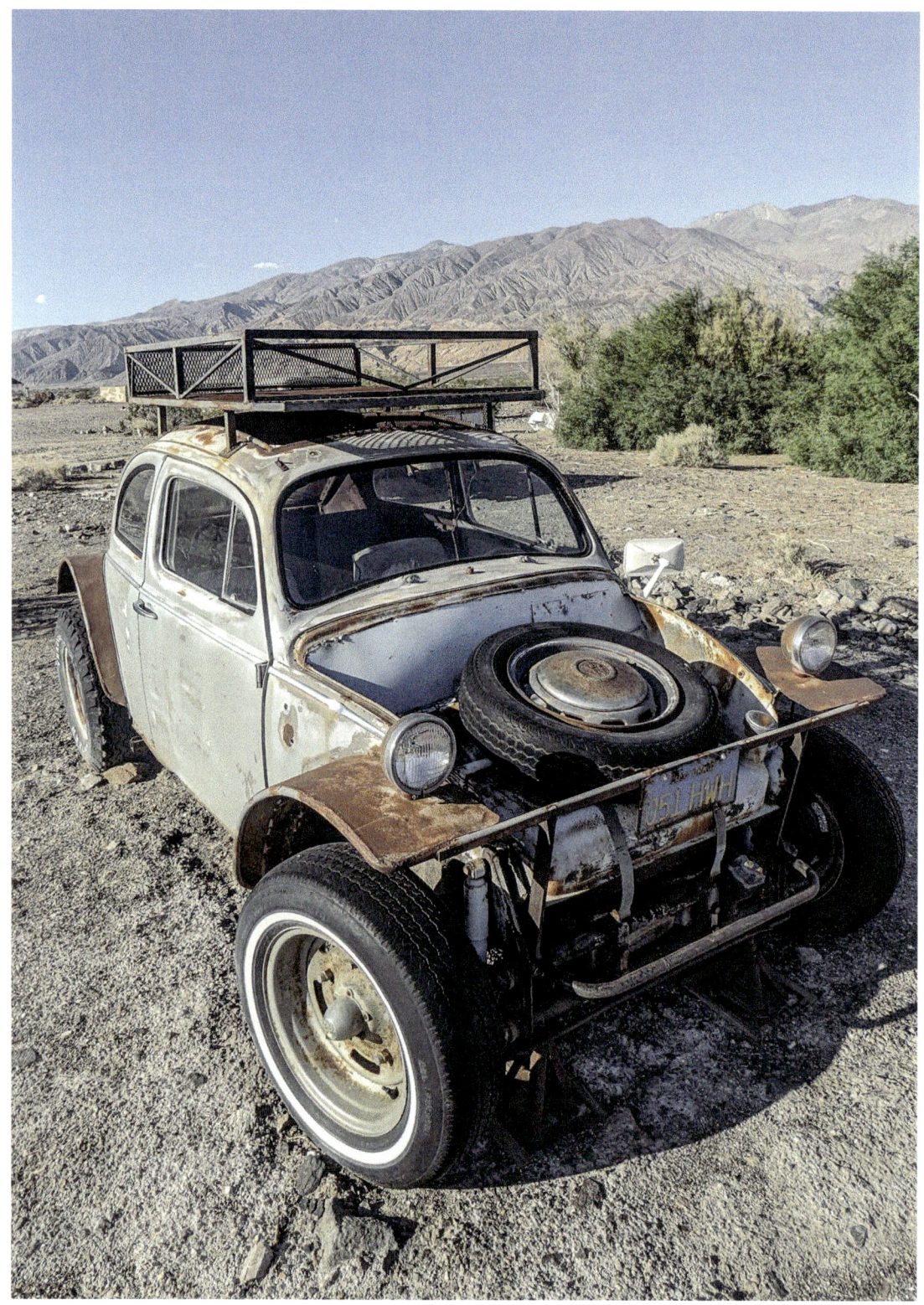

Volkswagen dune buggy.

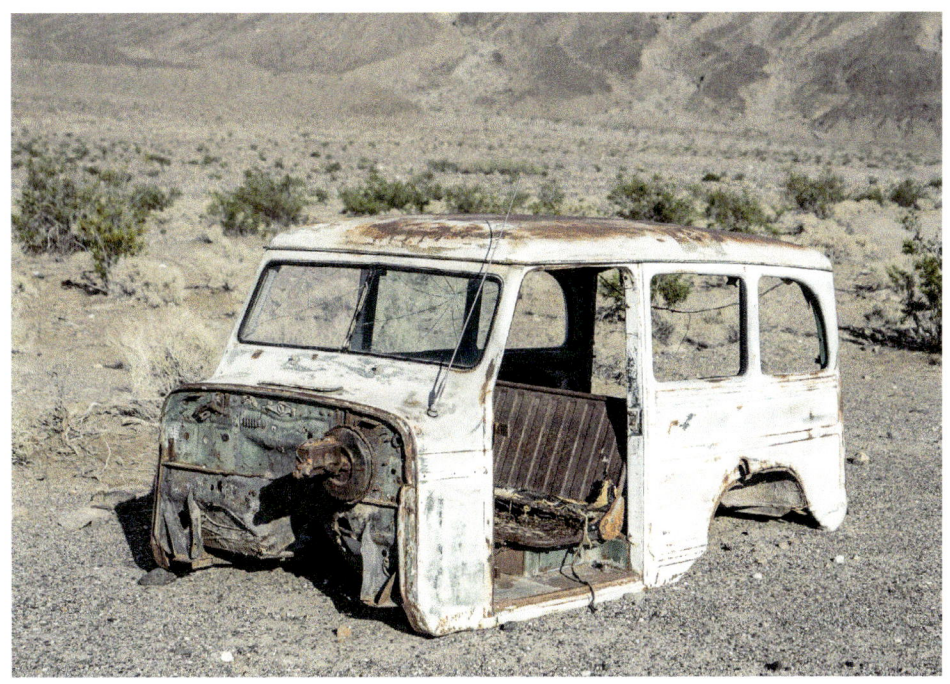

Car body, with the Panamint mountain range in the background.

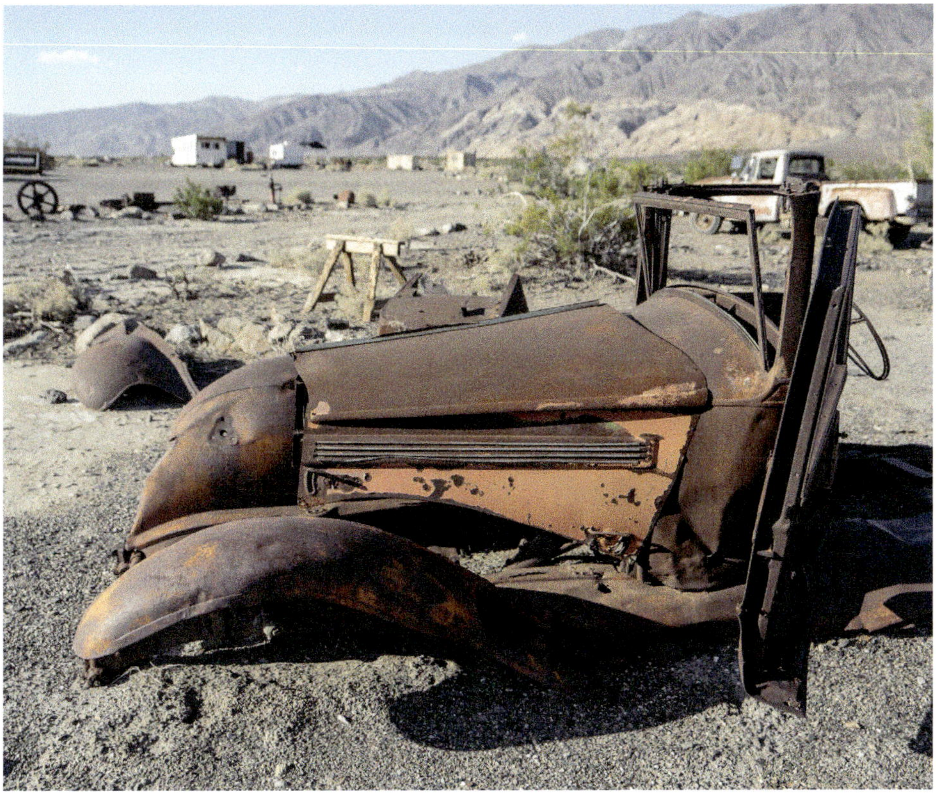

Rusted car remains.

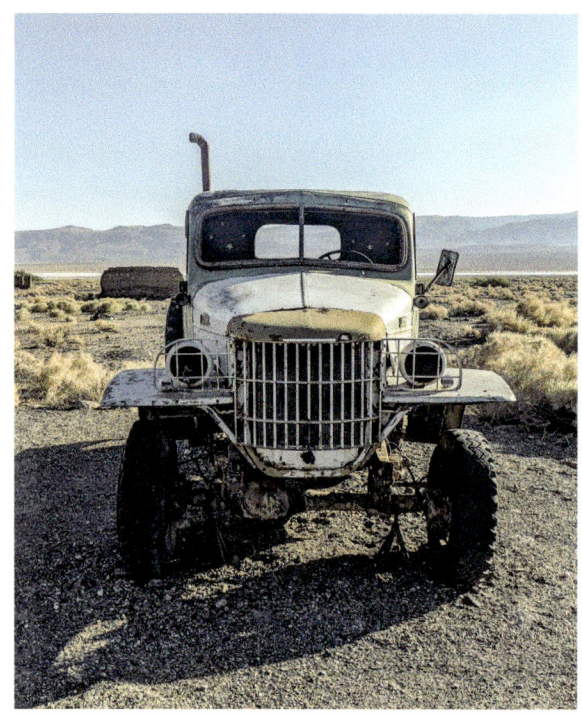

Left: "The Manson Family Truck." If you look closely, you can see the stars on the interior of the cab.

Below: The Manson Family left their mark on this truck, parked in the town of Ballerat.

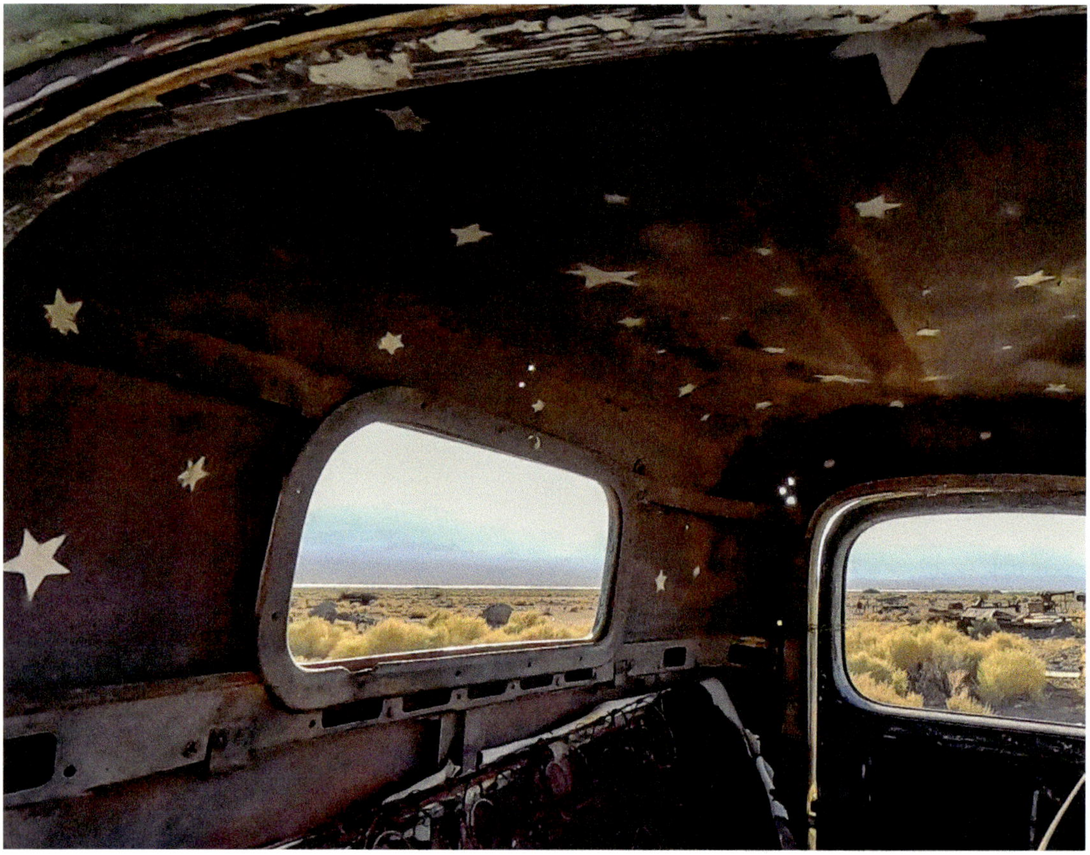

8

THE SAND HOUSES: A NEIGHBORHOOD WHERE THE ELEMENTS WON

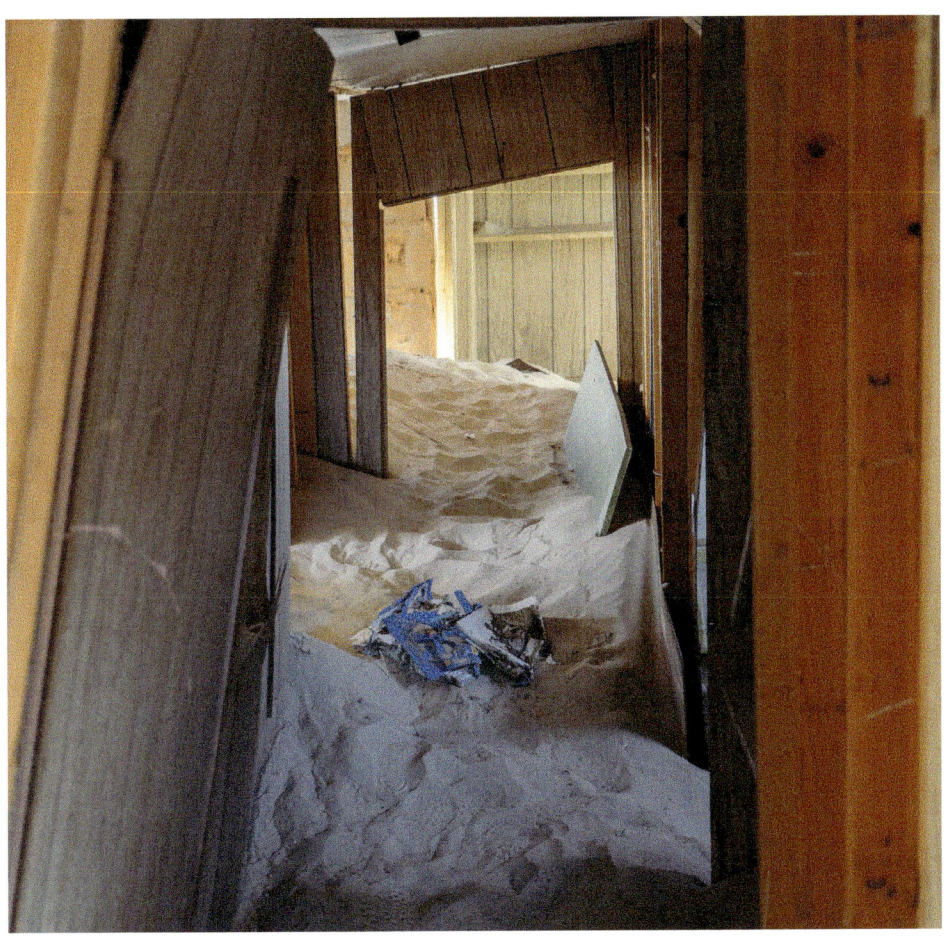

The hallway of a house, overtaken by drifting sand.

Nestled along the banks of the elusive Mojave River, a remote neighborhood in California once thrived amidst the arid beauty of its surroundings. The residents, drawn to the allure of a quiet life, found solace in a community woven into the fabric of the desert. For most of the year, the riverbed lay dry, a testament to the arid nature of the desert landscape.

The tranquility of this secluded neighborhood faced an unforeseen challenge. The narrow road, that connected the community to the outer world, crossed the riverbed. Occasionally, during large storms the river would deposit sand on the road. During the drier months the road suffered from drifting sands accumulating on the pavement, making it near impossible to pass. From 1979 to 1991, county maintenance crews diligently cleared the accumulating sand, depositing tons of it on the downwind side of the road. The intention was to prevent the sands from blowing back onto the road, ensuring the safety of the residents. However, the consequences rippled further than anticipated. Unbeknownst to the county maintenance crews, a community further downwind was bearing the brunt of this unforeseen consequence.

As the sands silently settled, the once-vibrant neighborhood found itself amid an environmental disaster. Homes and structures, once steadfast against the elements, began to succumb to the encroaching sands. Residents, faced with the relentless advance of the desert did everything they could to battle the incoming dunes. Some built retaining walls, while others purchased bulldozers and dump trucks to move the sand, making every effort to prevent its accumulation. The forces of nature become too much for several residents, as they were forced to abandon their homes, leaving behind the echoes of a life disrupted.

Several of the homeowners sued the county, demanding over $6 million in damages so they could relocate their homes. It is uncertain if they residents will receive compensation.

Today, the remnants of these abandoned houses stand as silent reminders, their windows gazing out across the shifting sands that have reclaimed what was once a vibrant community.

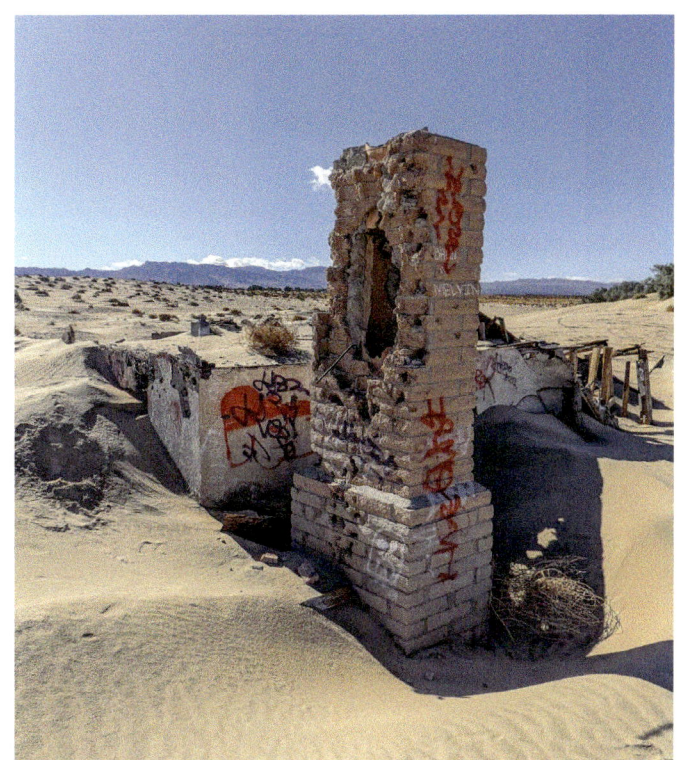

Right: The chimney and a few concrete walls are all that remain of this home.

Below: Rusted and mangled pieces of truck left behind when people moved on.

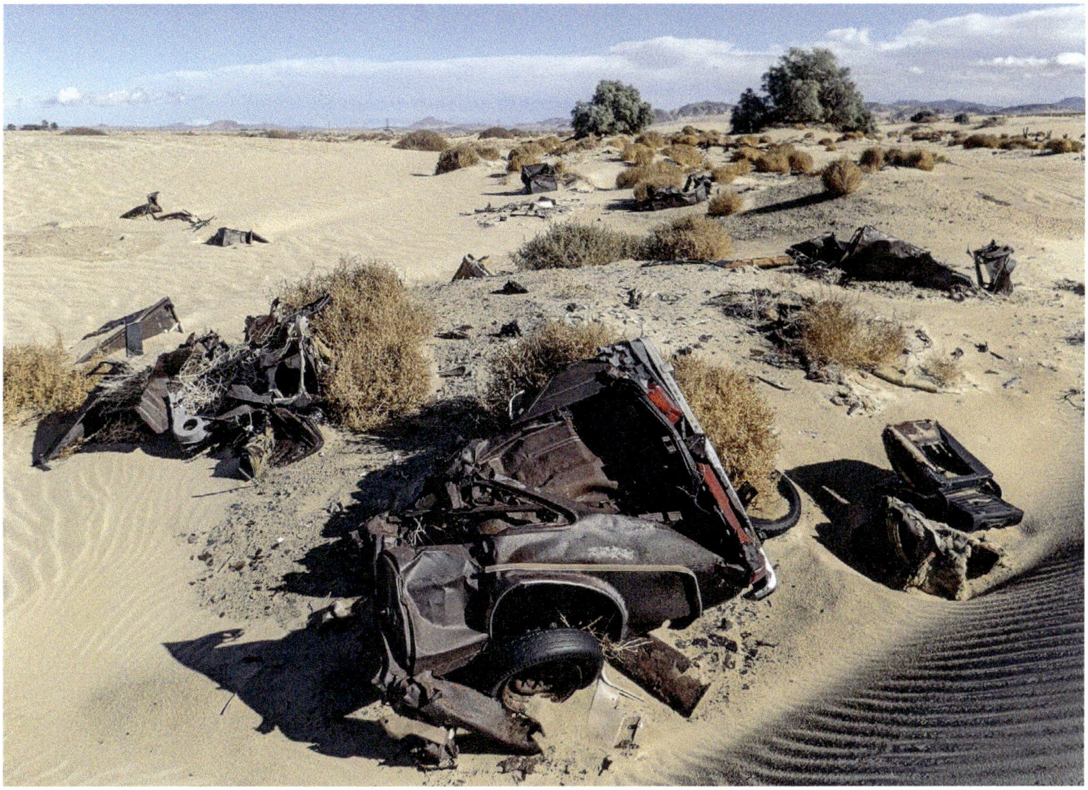

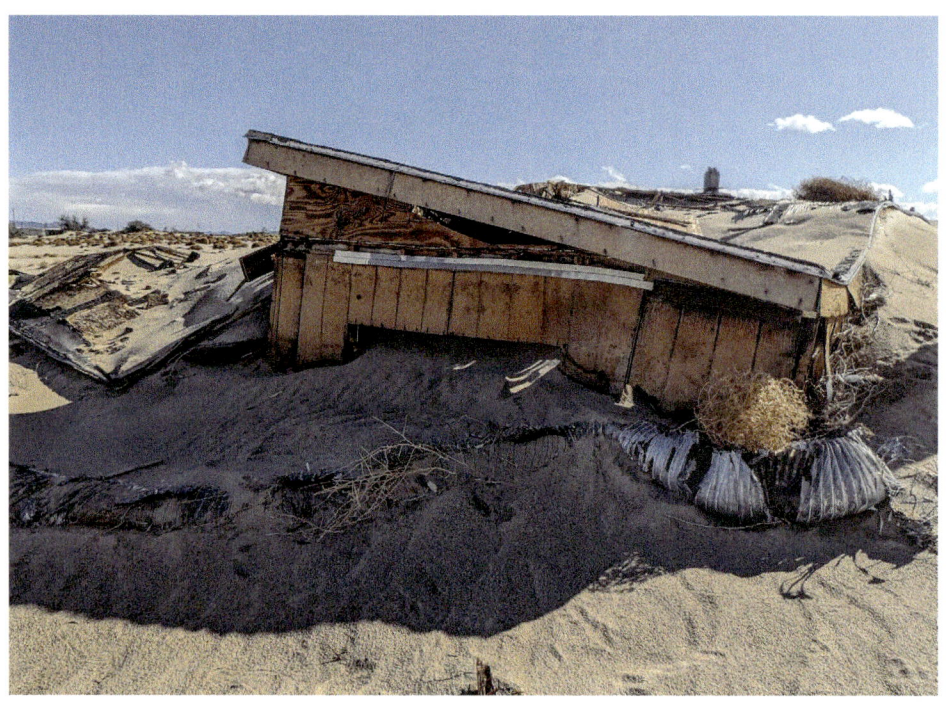

This building is almost completely covered by the drifting sands.

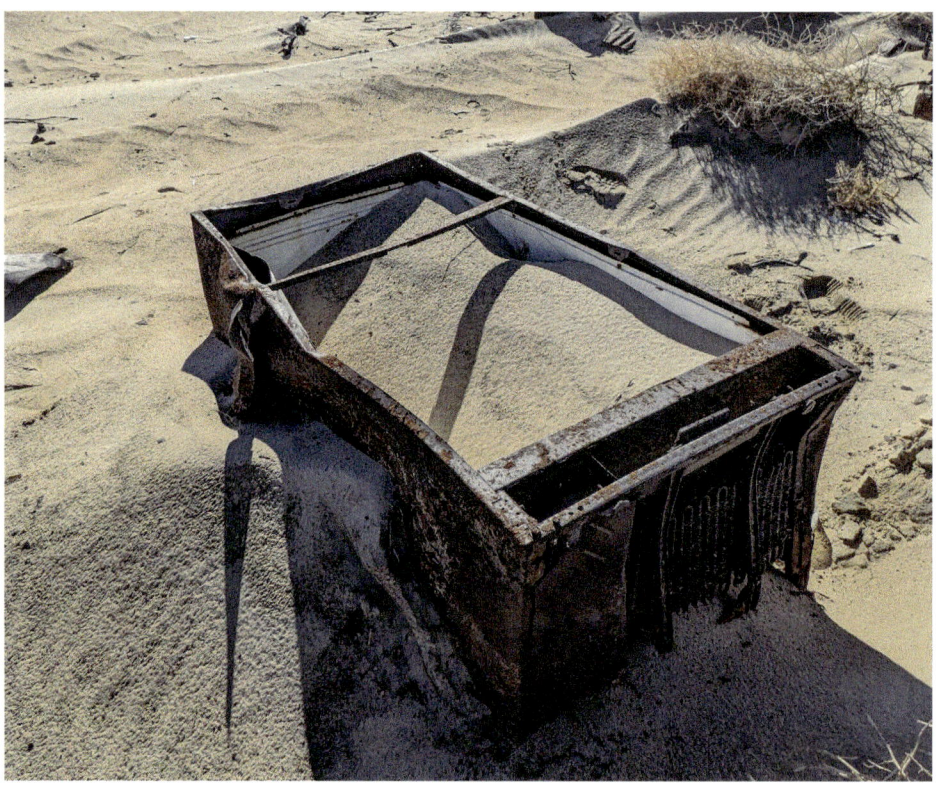

Rusted remains of a refrigerator.

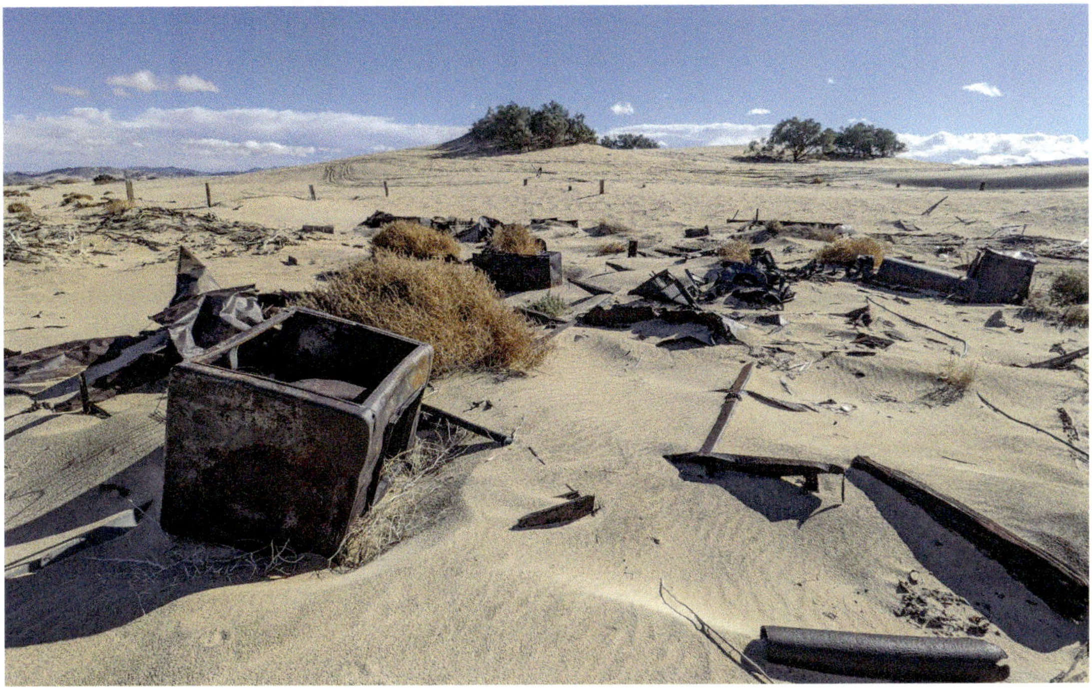

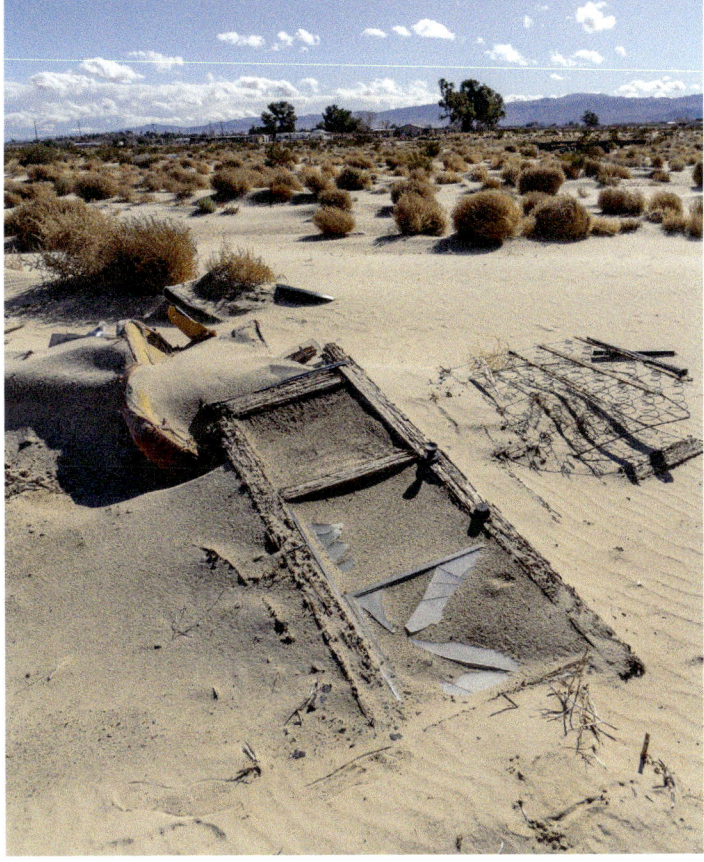

Above: Various belongings, metal and wood scattered across someone's former property.

Right: Doorframe, couch, and mattress springs.

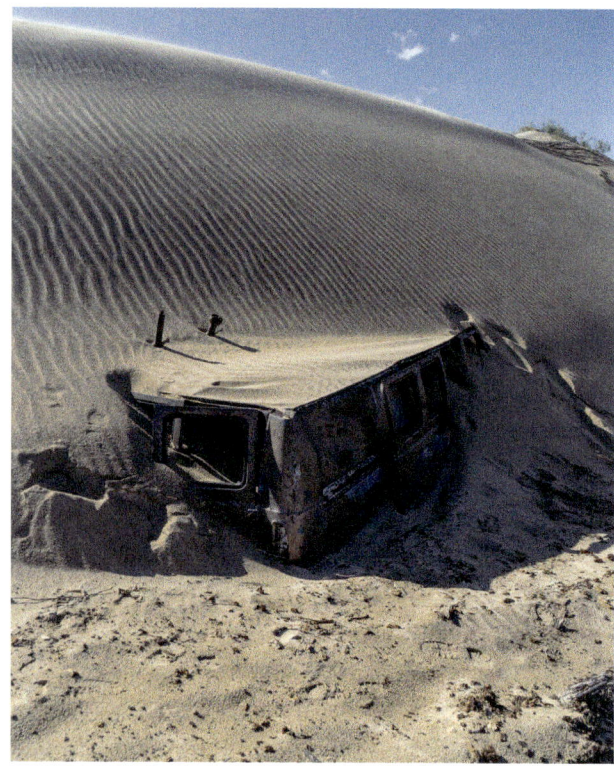

This van has been parked here for a long time.

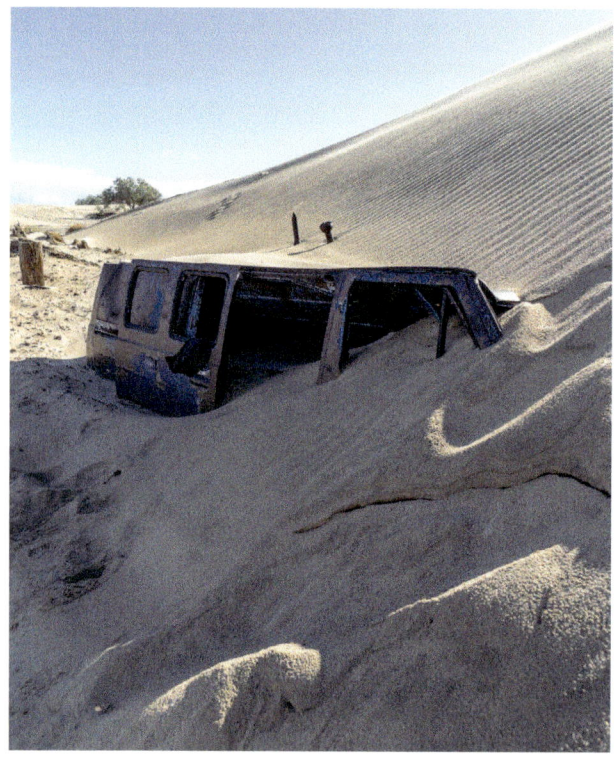

Almost completely engulfed in sand.

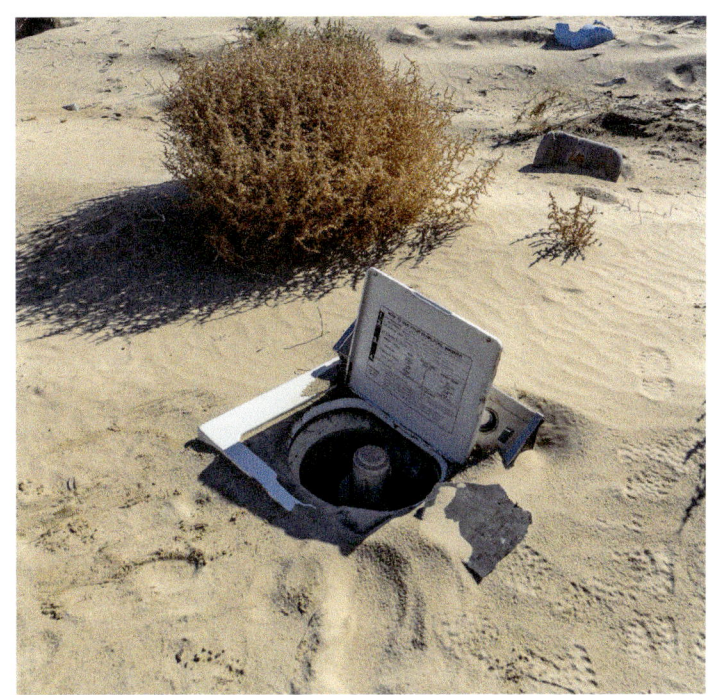

Right: A clothes washer, which is almost completely buried.

Below: Abandoned car.

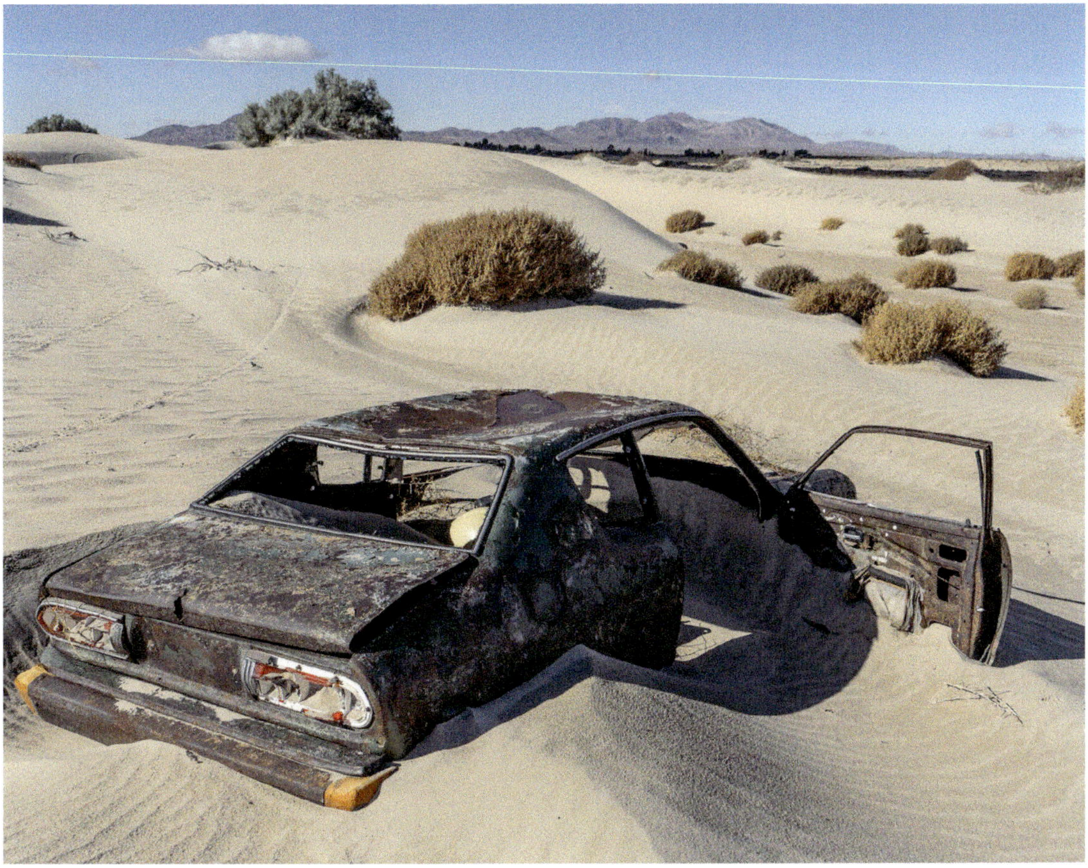

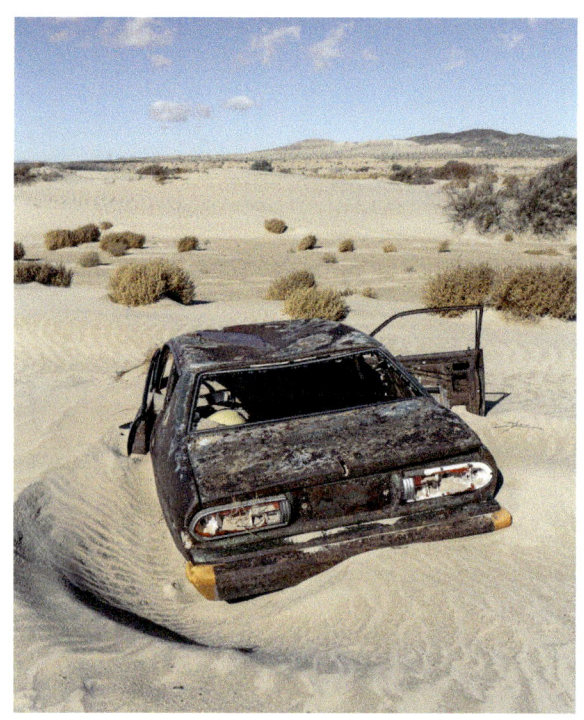

Left: A car standing on its own. It is possible there is a building here that is entirely covered in sand.

Below: House and garage. One of the most visible structures in this community.

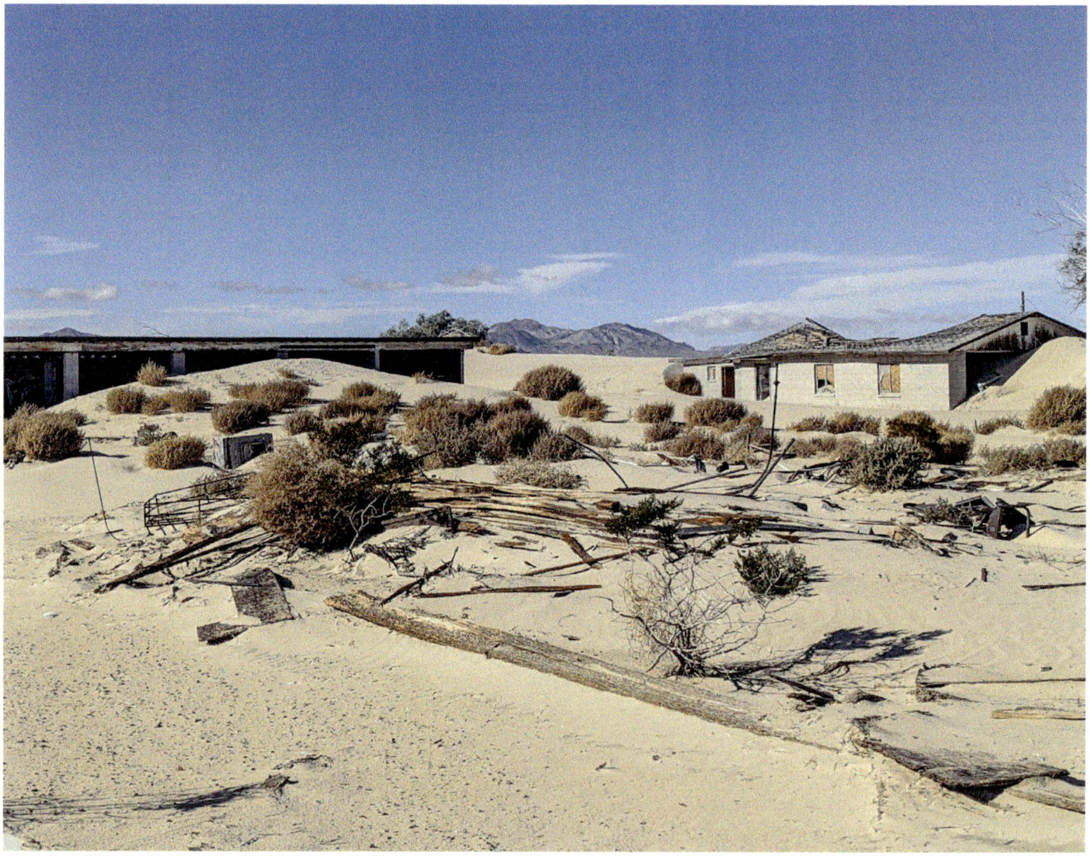

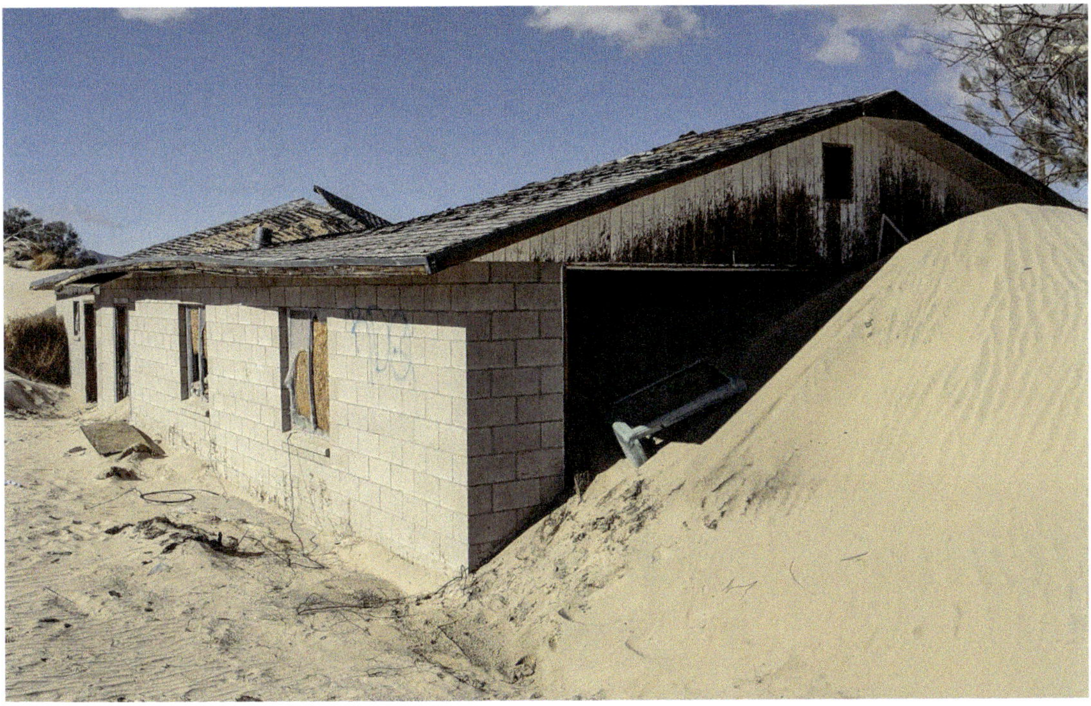

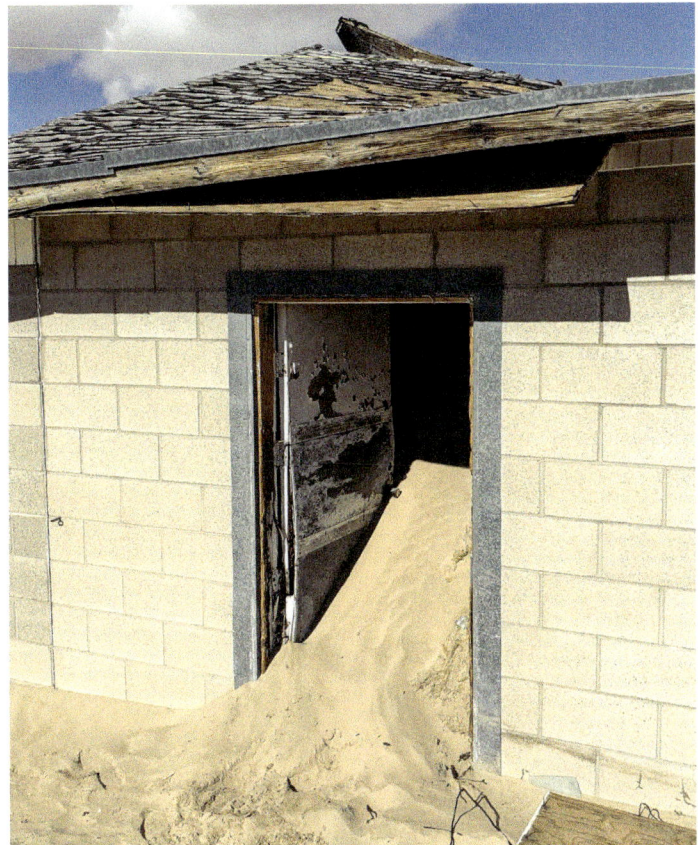

Above: The house.

Right: Sand has completely overtaken this house.

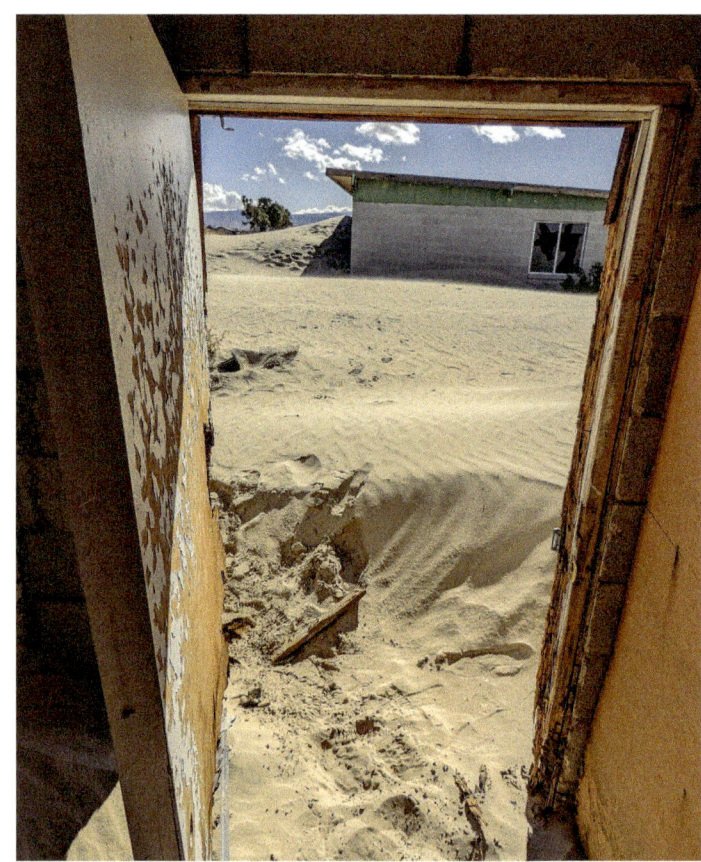

Left: Looking toward the garage.

Below: The roof has collapsed, accelerating the infiltration of the sand dunes.

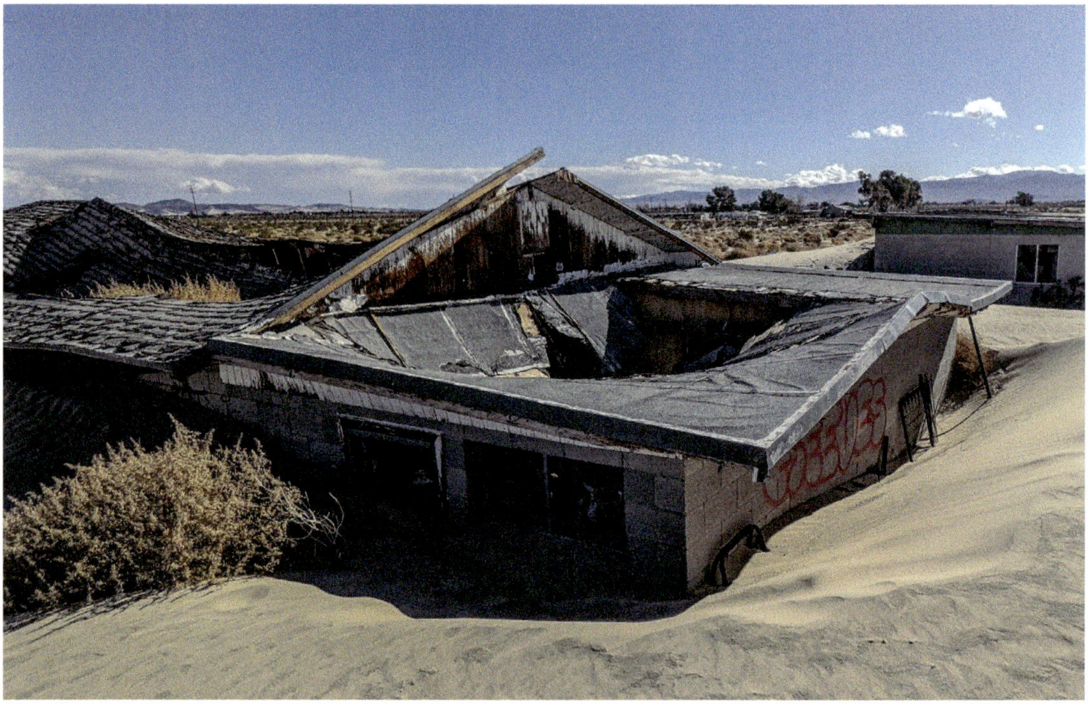

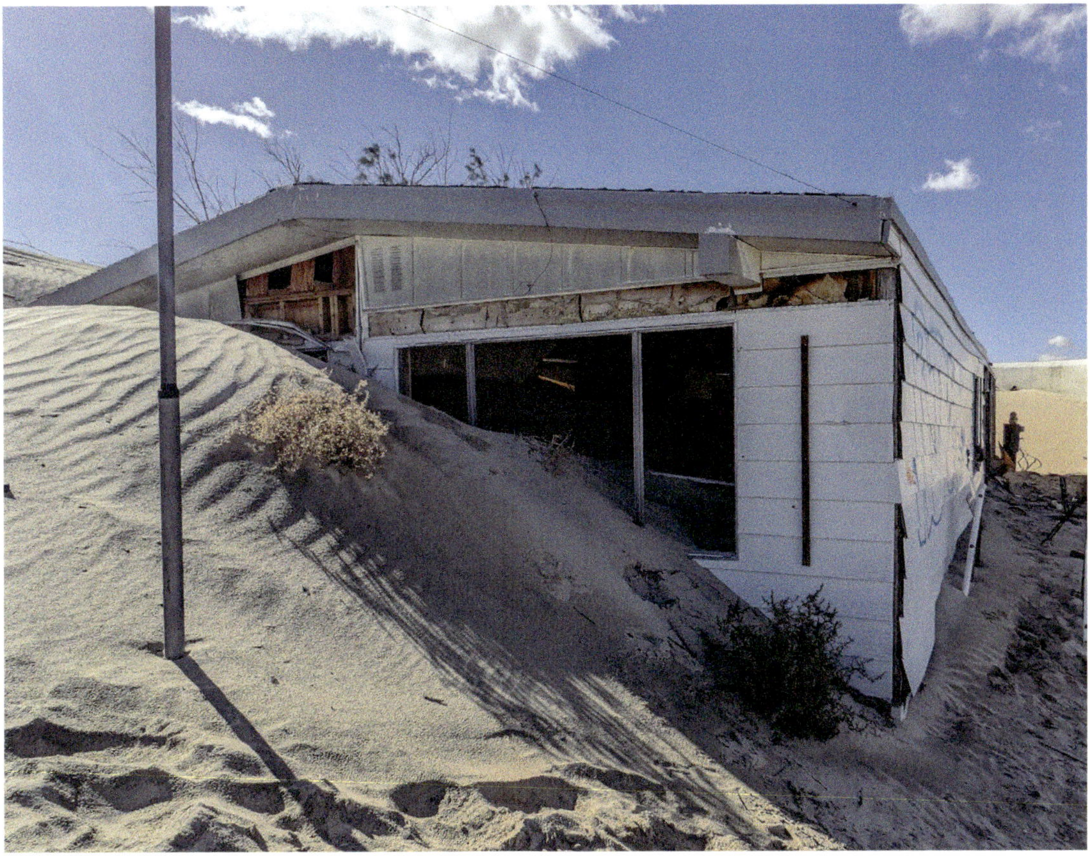

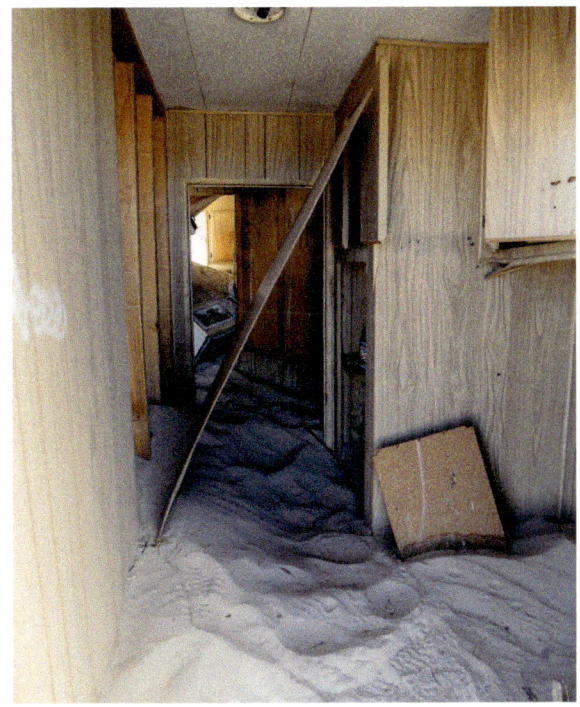

Above: Another home almost completely buried.

Right: Entrance to the home.

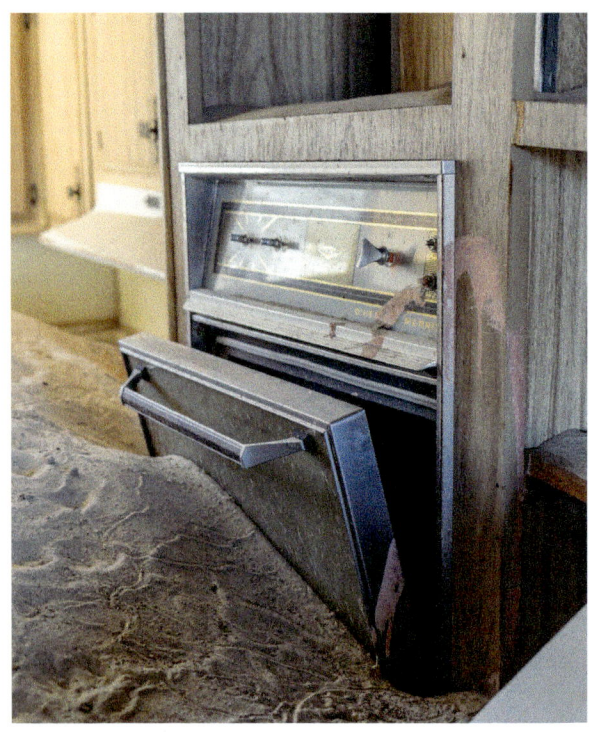

Left: The kitchen, with stove.

Below: Front gate to the home.

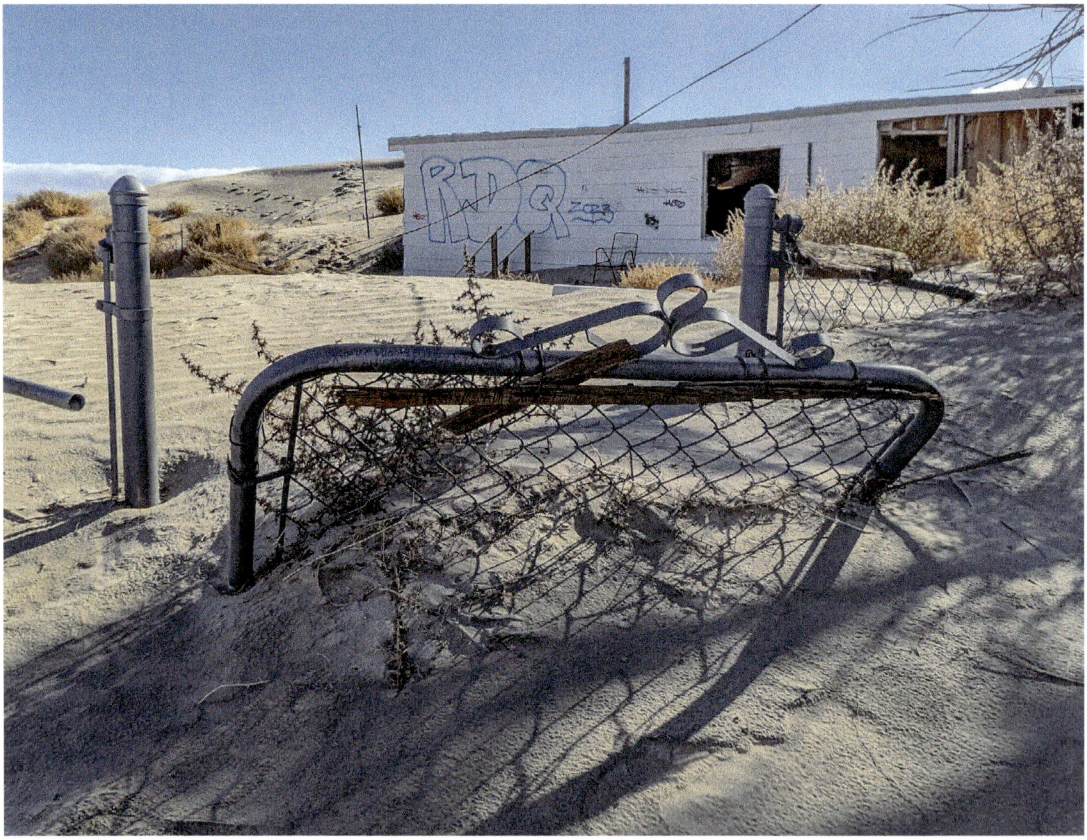

REFERENCES

www.newworldencyclopedia.org/entry/California

en.wikipedia.org/wiki/Eagle_Mountain,_California

en.wikipedia.org/wiki/Desert_Center,_California

en.wikipedia.org/wiki/Colorado_River_Aqueduct

en.wikipedia.org/wiki/San_Diego_and_Arizona_Eastern_Railway

www.hmdb.org/m.asp?m=193810

en.wikipedia.org/wiki/Goat_Canyon_Trestle

en.wikipedia.org/wiki/Lake_Dolores_Waterpark

www.vvdailypress.com/story/lifestyle/travel/2021/01/10/
    beyers-byways-lake-dolores-past-present-and-future/6593389002/

stuckeys.com/motel-monday-arnes-royal-hawaiian-baker-ca/

en.wikipedia.org/wiki/Ballarat,_California

www.latimes.com/archives/la-xpm-1993-05-24-mn-39321-story.html

ABOUT THE AUTHOR

Kevin Lacy, a native of Western New York State, has called California home since 2014. Kevin's career as a professional photographer has taken him all over the world, but he has always been drawn to the California desert. Over the past decade, he has been on an artistic journey to document the stark beauty, resilience, and enchantment of this captivating landscape. His work resonates with those who appreciate the delicate interplay of light and shadow in the arid wilderness, encapsulating the essence of the desert's allure, and the beauty of its decaying structures in this unforgiving environment.